INDIE AUTHOR MAGAZINE

HELLO AND WELCOME!

I'm Indie Annie, and I'm thrilled you're reading this gorgeous full-color version of IAM. Did you know that you can also access all the information, education, and inspiration in our app? It's available on both the iOS App Store and Google Play. And for those that prefer to listen to me read articles, you can pop over to Spotify or our website. Happy Reading!

X

IndieAuthorMagazine.com

Download on the
App Store

GET IT ON
Google Play

GOAL SETTING

INDiE AUTHOR MAGAZINE

Volume 2 • Issue 12 • December 2022

GOAL SETTING

This Issue's Featured Author: MARK DAWSON

Q&A: Indie Author Experts Reflect on Industry Growth and Where We're Headed in 2023

7 Steps to Your Perfect Five-Year Publishing Plan

10 Tips for Choosing Your Perfect Planner

Making the List: A Multi-Time Bestseller Recounts Her Road to the Top

How Spicy Romance Authors Turn up the Heat for Readers

ON THE COVER

INDIE
AUTHOR MAGAZINE

PUBLISHER
Chelle Honiker

CREATIVE DIRECTOR
Alice Briggs

EDITOR IN CHIEF
Nicole Schroeder

COPY EDITOR
Lisa Thompson

WRITERS
Angela Archer
Elaine Bateman
Patricia Carr
Bradley Charbonneau
Laurel Decher
Fatima Fayez
Gill Fernley
Greg Fishbone
Chrishaun Keller-Hanna
Jac Harmon
Marion Hermannsen
Audrey Hughey

WRITERS
Liv Honeywell
Kasia Lasinska
Megan Linski-Fox
Bre Lockhart
Sìne Màiri MacDougall
Angie Martin
Merri Maywether
Kevin McLaughlin
Susan Odev
Jenn Mitchell
Clare Sager
Nicole Schroeder
Emilia Zeeland

PUBLISHER
Athenia Creative
6820 Apus Dr.
Sparks, NV, 89436 USA
775.298.1925

ISSN 2768-7880 (online)–ISSN 2768-7872 (print)

From the Publisher

At the recent 20Booksto50K® conference in Las Vegas, it was a great pleasure to meet with many colleagues and friends at our vendor booth. I've said that it feels less like the largest indie author conference in the world and more like a family reunion.

Along with the camaraderie we enjoyed all week with old and new friends, it was an opportunity to answer questions I'm often asked. This month, I thought I would answer them here as well.

Q. How do you choose who is on the cover?
1   It's a combination of a few things, but it isn't a strict recipe. Each issue has a theme, and sometimes our featured subject embodies the theme. The common criteria is an inspirational story. We love to share the stories of authors—or couples, like Dr. Danielle and Dakota Krout—who define success on their own terms and reach back to help others.

Q. Who should read Indie Author Magazine?
1   Our tagline is "When Writing Means Business." I would say that if you have a goal to make money from your writing, whether you want to write full time or as a hobby, then IAM is for you.

Q. Where can I read Indie Author Magazine?
1   Here's a fun fact: Each month, we publish exactly how a wide author does. We use our website to manage e-book subscriptions and deliver them via BookFunnel. We also publish e-books via Amazon and Draft2Digital, so they're available in all the major retailers. We publish print versions via Amazon.com and IngramSpark, as well as Lulu.com, and dropship them to our print subscribers. We also push articles to our iOS and Google Play apps, along with a print color PDF version and an audio version of each article. We have a podcast on Spotify, Google Podcast, Amazon Music, Spotify, and Stitcher.

There's nothing quite like the energy and enthusiasm of in-person chats, and we're planning to attend more conferences in 2023. We hope to see you in person soon, and until then, we wish everyone a healthy and happy holiday season and new year.

CHELLE HONIKER

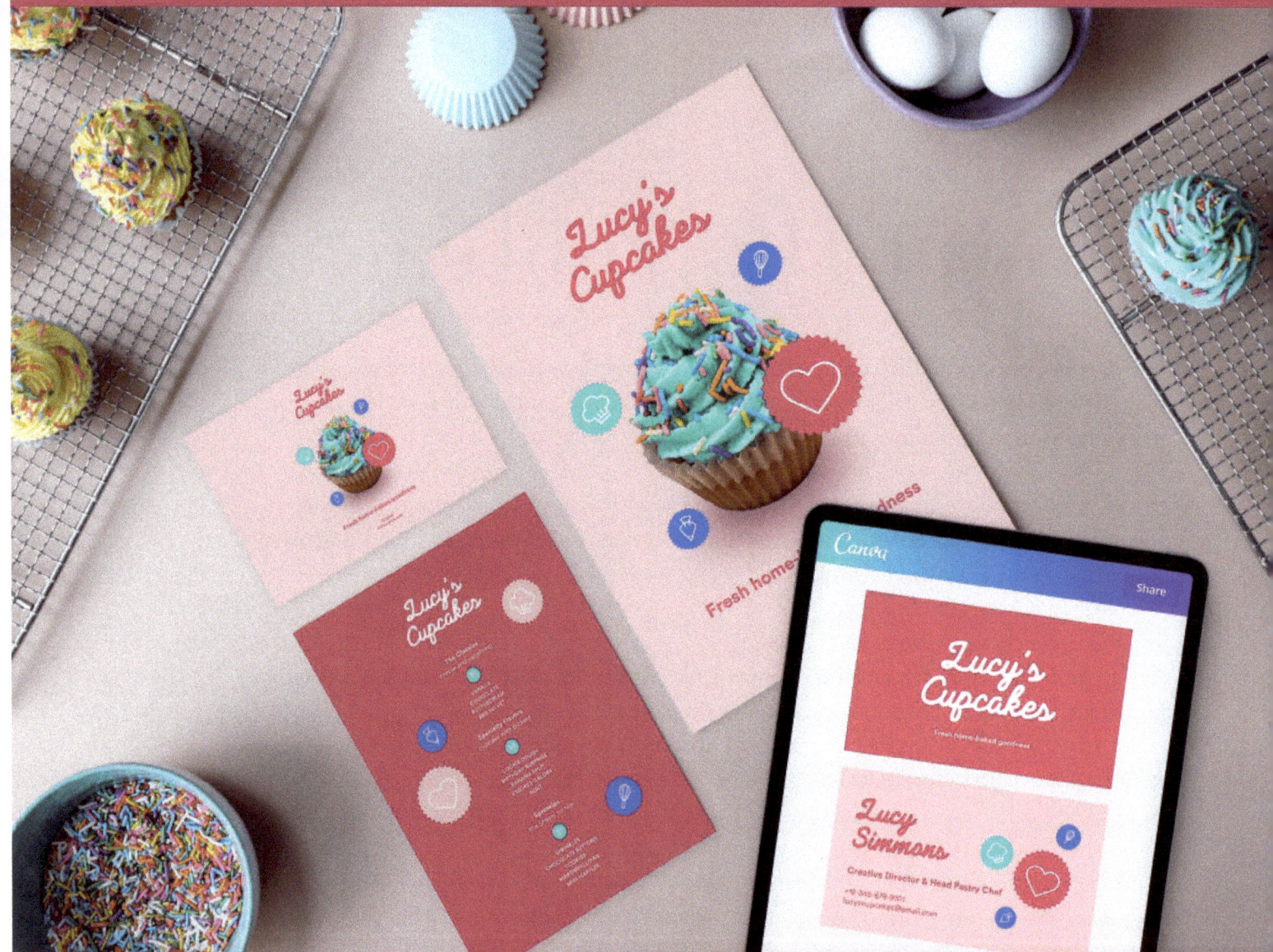

Design like a Pro for free

From the Editor in Chief

One of my favorite parts of Christmas morning has always been reading the letter Santa Claus leaves for me and my siblings.

My parents started the tradition when I was around five years old. Every year, we'd wake up to a letter that talked about everything we'd each accomplished that year and how proud we'd made our parents. I remember when I was younger, I would sneak out of bed and try to read it before anyone else, glancing only briefly at the presents under the tree before shining a flashlight across the official-looking "From the Desk of Santa Claus" letterhead. It was—and still is—my favorite of our family traditions around the holidays, and now that I know it's my dad adopting the pen name, it only feels more special.

One thing I like most about these letters is the chance to reminisce and reflect. In all the rush of the holiday season, it's easy to look past just how much you've accomplished in the past year. That's why this month, I wanted to share my family's holiday tradition with you. Besides, I might not have access to the North Pole's fancy stationery, but what kind of journalist would I be if I weren't willing to share a message from an important public figure with our readers?

"Indie author, what a year it's been! Bringing new books to life for your readers, connecting with other authors at conferences, teaching yourself how to use new platforms and technology. You've taken on about as much work as me this year, and that's saying something, ho ho ho! The elves tell me you've been working hard on some new story ideas as well. I hope you're not planning on making things too difficult for your characters. I don't know if we can take another cliffhanger like that last one! On a serious note, I know the work can be frustrating and stressful at times, but always remember, you're chasing your dreams and proving yourself to the world. Writing isn't easy, but that's even more reason to be so proud of what you've accomplished. Your readers adore your books—I wish I could show you just how many are already wrapped and waiting in my sleigh!—and we can't wait to see what you have in store next year."

From all of us at *Indie Author Magazine*, have a happy holiday season and a wonderful new year.

Nicole Schroeder
Editor in Chief
Indie Author Magazine

You Don't Know What You Don't Know

When you have no books published, what does a launch strategy look like?

This is a question I have been asked at every stop so far on the epic 20Books Drive Across America and the profound train ride around the UK.

From a strategic perspective, you don't know how your book will be received. You probably aren't sure of the exact genre (for marketing purposes). You aren't sure of the technical process of publishing. There are so many things that you don't know, but there is one simple way to get some of that information: Publish your book. You don't have to build a readership before you have anything for them to read. You don't have to set up blog tours or promotions. You don't have to do any of that.

And too many people think that you do, and it is holding them back. I think the people I've met were looking for a strategy that included joining feedback groups, setting up a newsletter, running promotions—those things that seasoned authors will do to launch their books. They built that stuff over a long period of time. They have existing readers, also built over time.

It takes bait to attract the fish. No one dangles a bare hook and expects to catch anything. With a product, you now have the means to attract readers—those people who might like your style and read your books.

Until you publish, you don't know what you don't know, but you can always sell a good book. You may end up putting a new cover on it. You will redo the blurb. You may even rewrite it. Nothing is fatal for an author's career. We learn, and we grow.

Would it be better to have a reader magnet first? In your overall sales funnel, yes, having a reader magnet—short story to full-

length book, the best sample of your style that you can manage—is beneficial, but you'll run across the same problems. How do you get it into readers' hands? If you have the magnet ready, publish it. If you don't, publish the book, and at some point in the future, get the reader magnet into the mix.

Consider the chicken and the egg. Start learning what you don't know by using what you have at hand. One of my bestselling books this year is one I published five and a half years ago to no audience, without a readership, with a bad cover, and I could go on, but why? When the third book in that series was ready with new covers on them all, I ran promotions on book one, and that started a great five-year run that has led to over one hundred thousand dollars in sales for that series.

Getting it right before you know anything about this business is putting a great deal of pressure on yourself. Getting it right eventually is an effective way to launch a career. The best thing you can do to help yourself is to get the book out there and listen to the feedback. And keep in mind that nothing sells your first book like the newest book. Write another book, and write it better.

Craig Martelle

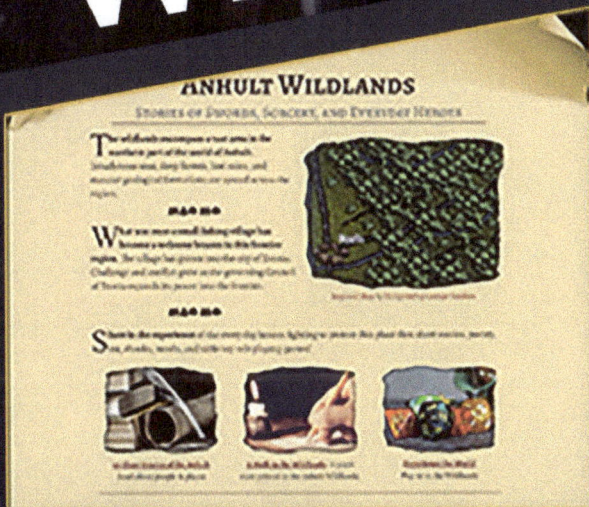

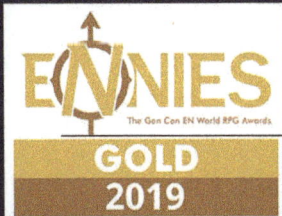

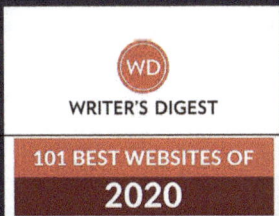

Dear Indie Annie,

I started to write a fairy-tale retelling, but it has morphed into something more Sci-Fi. Do I let the story run away with me? Or do I force it to stick to my plan?

Lost the Plot in Lajas

DEAR LOST,

How are you, my lovely? Well, I hope, because it sounds like you have been having a lot of fun at your book's expense.

But let's park that idea for a moment. Have you heard of Eurovision? The Euro-vision Song Contest is a much-loved world-wide musical phenomenon. I am sure our readers in Europe and even Australia are throwing their sequined sleeves in the air right now, screaming, "Indie Annie, we know where you're going with this!" Because when they read your question, they too will have had a particular song running through their heads, and I guess they will also struggle to shake it off. It's infectious. It's Alexander Rybak's master-piece "Fairytale."

Rybak became a household name across Europe after winning the Grand Final of the 2009 Eurovision Song Contest for Norway with 387 points out of a possible 492, the highest-recorded score in the contest's history. "Fairytale" went on to top the charts in many European coun-tries, and the follow-up album, *Fairytales*, was released in twenty-five countries. This was quite an achievement, especially for an entry from Norway, which holds the record for the country with the most zero-point entries in history. (For fact-checkers: They scored nil points four times, in 1963, 1978, 1981, and 1997.)

"Indie Annie," I hear you cry, "why, oh why, are you talking about a song called 'Fairytale' when I am telling you I am struggling to keep on track with my retelling as it is? I don't need to go any further off-piste!" And, my dear Lost, I hear you; I truly do. All I ask is that you defer from heading off to Spotify or YouTube to listen to this wonderful

Need help from your favorite Indie Aunt?
Ask Dear Indie Annie a question at
IndieAnnie@indieauthormagazine.com

little song for a few minutes whilst I explain my thinking to you.

When "Fairytale" won, it was an instant smash. I can recall I was in London with friends at the time. They throw an annual Eurovision party and watch the television show live. They eat food from the countries taking part. They have individual scorecards and vote for their own favorites. It's great fun. I have taken part in this yearly celebration of music a couple of times, and this was the first year everyone agreed on the winner.

Rybak was fresh faced, doe eyed, and could play the violin better than the devil who went down to Georgia. In a sea of Europop blandness, he went back to basics and crafted a simple song that pulled the audience into his love story with the toe-tapping accompaniment of his country's traditional folk music. Others copied him in the years that followed, but no one has recaptured that magic.

What has this to do with your question? My dear, the answer is in your chosen genre. Why do people read fairy-tale retellings? Because the stories are timeless. They work because at their core we recognize the stories of our forebears: the legends, the myths, the tales before bedtime. A retelling places these much-loved stories in a different world, usually by making them more contemporary. Rybak did the same. He knew that the sound of the violin would tug at our universal heartstrings. His words described falling in love with the perfect person as not a blessing but a curse—one that, if we are lucky, will drive us all insane. And being madly in love is what we all desire. It calls to our deepest fears and secret longings.

Fairy tales do the same. So if your story has been transported to a galaxy far, far away, perhaps there is an audience waiting there to read it. Your choice is to decide whether you want to boldly go where no writer has gone before or revisit what you have written so far and bring it back down to earth. I cannot answer that conundrum for you, but Norway and Rybak took a risk, and it paid off handsomely. Be bold. Be brave. Be you.

Happy Writing,
Indie Annie

10 TIPS FOR
CHOOSING YOUR PERFECT PLANNER

Planners can be an excellent investment of your time and money, helping you create effective goals and build actionable plans. But with so many options available, it's important to research which planner will work best for your unique writing life. Ahead of the new year, we're breaking down ten things every author should keep in mind when selecting a planner so they can stay organized in their author business and beyond.

1 CONSIDER YOUR MEDIUM

When reviewing planners, consider which form of technology will best suit your preferences while encouraging good planning habits. Although pen and paper are a must for some, others prefer to go fully digital. It's also possible to combine both physical and digital planners.

Pro Tip: The adage "Out of sight, out of mind" is especially true when it comes to planners, no matter which format you pick. If you select a paper planner, try to keep it on your desk or where you can lay it open in your writing space. This ensures you're reminded to use it regularly. For those who choose a digital option, set reminders on your phone or computer to look at your planner so you're clear on what you need to accomplish each day.

2 CREATE YOUR OWN PAPER PLANNER ...

A variety of programs and software allow authors to create their own planners and print them at stores like Office Depot or using print-on-demand service providers like LuLu Press. Canva can be an intuitive and easy-to-use platform for formatting a custom planner that will fit your needs, and you can even order your design directly from the site when you're finished.

3 ... CUSTOMIZE A NOTEBOOK OR JOURNAL ...

Another hands-on and affordable option for creating a custom paper planner is to purchase a notebook or journal and design your own unique pages. Incorporate designs that will help you create systems and habits, such as monthly calendars and habit trackers, and don't be afraid to adjust your planning system as the year progresses to make something that works for you.

Pro Tip: Bullet journaling and notebooks are not for everyone. Although there are thousands of blog posts, websites, and videos dedicated to bullet journaling, it's important to consider whether it's suitable for you. Consider your propensity for perfectionism when creating something from scratch that will often include artistic expression and require a time investment to create pages for what will essentially become a handmade planner. If perfectionism is not an issue for you and you're sure that you won't spend an inordinate amount of time creating them, then it could be an excellent option for creating a planning system unique to your life.

4 ... OR BUILD A DIGITAL PLANNER

With programs as straightforward and accessible as PowerPoint and Keynote, authors who prefer a digital option can create their own hyperlinked planners for use on tablets or in programs like OneNote, GoodNotes, and Notability. Build the journal on your own, or pull from tutorials online, including graphic designer Jet Sy's video tutorial walking users through the formatting process for Keynote on her YouTube channel, Jet Sy Traveling Designer.

5 CONSIDER INSPIRATION

When searching for your perfect planner, pay attention to layouts and interior designs that inspire you. With the right systems in place for planning, you can harness that inspiration and carry it with you throughout the year. Remember that each writer has different needs, motivations, and aspirations. The best planner for you is one that not only inspires you to plan but to keep it up long term for the best possible results.

6 VALUE FUNCTION OVER AESTHETICS

The physical and digital shelves of stores are filled to bursting with beautiful, exciting planners. Unfortunately, the desk drawers and closets of many well-intentioned writers are filled with pretty planners that were never used to their fullest potential. Choose a planner that fulfills your planning needs in form and function first, and beauty as a far second.

Pro Tip: Style isn't the most important aspect of selecting a planner, but it is still worth consideration. When you enjoy seeing your planner because you love the style, you are more likely to bring it along to writing events and keep it on top of your workspace instead of in a drawer.

7 BALANCE PRICE WITH FUNCTION

In some seasons of life, we bootstrap more than others, and in difficult economic climates, it's imperative to be mindful of how you spend your money. But keep in mind that many planners cover a twelve-month period and cost far less over the course of a year than the amount we may spend on other incidentals, such as video streaming services, quick runs to your favorite shop, a junk food habit, clothing subscriptions, or other disposable income draws. There are many places where you can and should save money, but don't skimp on your planner. Get the one you are most inspired to start—and keep—using. Remember to divide its cost by the number of months the planner covers to gain more perspective on the value provided.

8 CREATE A PLANNING SCHEDULE

Half of the battle of using a planner to its fullest potential is to use it consistently. As soon as you choose a planner, create a schedule for quarterly, monthly, and weekly planning and review sessions. Decide on that schedule, and enter it as a non-negotiable appointment in your new planner on the applicable dates.

Pro Tip: Use reminders on your phone or calendar to reinforce your commitment to the planning schedule you've created.

9 MIND YOUR TIME

Planning can be both fun and inspiring because it encourages us to tap into our desires and dreams. But planning should always be an effective investment of your most finite resource—time—and have a positive return on investment. If you spend so much time planning that you begin to use it as an excuse to procrastinate, the benefits of planning are significantly mitigated. Any time spent planning should be far less than the time you spend taking focused action that results in progress toward your most meaningful goals.

10 LIVE THE CHANGE YOU WANT TO SEE IN YOUR LIFE

As you're aiming for the next level of success in your authorship, think critically about exactly which parts of your life you wish to improve. Instead of waiting for a number, title, or milestone to begin embodying that next level of professionalism, incorporate those behaviors immediately. Ask yourself: How does that higher level of myself plan his or her writing and publishing schedule for the coming year? How does he or she build systems and habits for success? How does he or she invest in his or her writing career? How does he or she ensure he or she is making the best investment of his or her time, energy, and financial resources? Use your answers to set reminders to use your planner and to schedule regular planning and implementation sessions. ◼

Audrey Hughey

Frankfurt Book Fair Showcases a Bigger World for Indie Authors

Going to the Frankfurt Book Fair is a jolt of adrenaline for book lovers.

For the past seventy-four years, from all the regions of the world, publishers have been coming together to show off their beautiful work for readers, and as an indie author, you are part of the trade. Each year, the six-plus buildings house the main events of the Olympics of publishing, and any author whose inspiration is flagging will surely benefit from riding up the escalators and strolling the skyways and courtyard, where the action takes place.

The massiveness of the fair is also the biggest challenge. Because it is so big, other organizations nest their annual meetings inside it: receptions, readings, #BookTok in the outside courtyard called the Agora, and an event called BOOKFEST, an international cultural festival that's free to the public. At this year's event, held October 19–23, 93,000 trade visitors came to buy and sell rights for books, and 87,000 visitors from the general public came to watch the pageantry, according to a press release issued by event organizers.

This year's theme was "translation," and the King and Queen of Spain opened the fair after a year in which the translation market for Spanish books boomed. President Volodymyr Zelenkskyy of Ukraine also presented at the fair, appealing to attendees in his six-minute recorded speech to fight against terrorism. "Keep writing about it. Keep reading about it," he said. "Create, publish, and distribute books." There were exhibitor stands for ninety-five countries—from Canada to Malaysia—because books are a way to talk to each other across political and geographic borders. Fair organizers have already announced Slovenia as next year's guest of honor.

For those who are interested in watching the book Olympics from home, the Publishing Perspectives newsletter has been covering the

Frankffurter Buchmesse/Anett Weirauch

Frankffurter Buchmesse/Anett Weirauch

fair in English since 2009, according to its website. Download this year's fair magazine at https://publishingperspectives.com/frankfurt-book-fair-2022/#magazine, or subscribe to the organization's newsletter at https://publishingperspectives.com/subscribe/.

It'll make you proud to be part of it all.

FRANKFURT AS RIGHTS FAIR

If you thought the number of books published every day on Amazon was daunting, you can feel truly invisible—and excluded—in Frankfurt. How will readers find your work when there's so much to choose from? In addition to the massive volume of books, there are also still parts of the fair where self-published authors aren't permitted.

As an author or publisher, you can attend both the "trade" days, Wednesday through Thursday, and the public days, Friday and Saturday, of the event. Literary agents—three hundred in 2022—maintain a fortress in the LitAgerary Agents & Scout Centre (LitAg), where authors aren't admitted without an appointment made weeks or months in advance. The largest publishers' stands are full of small

tables and chairs, surrounded by shoulder-high walls displaying new releases. Inside these glowing corrals, agents and acquisition editors flip through book catalogs and negotiate deals. It's literary speed-dating.

If you are an illustrator, you might get close enough to show your portfolio, but as a humble wielder of words, you are confined to the remaining four thousand exhibitor stands, the outside courtyard called the Agora, the Congress Center, and various other venues in the city of Frankfurt.

Not to worry; the story isn't over yet.

FRANKFURT AS THOUGHT LEADER

If you ever thought there was only one way to publish a book, the Frankfurt Book Fair will cure you.

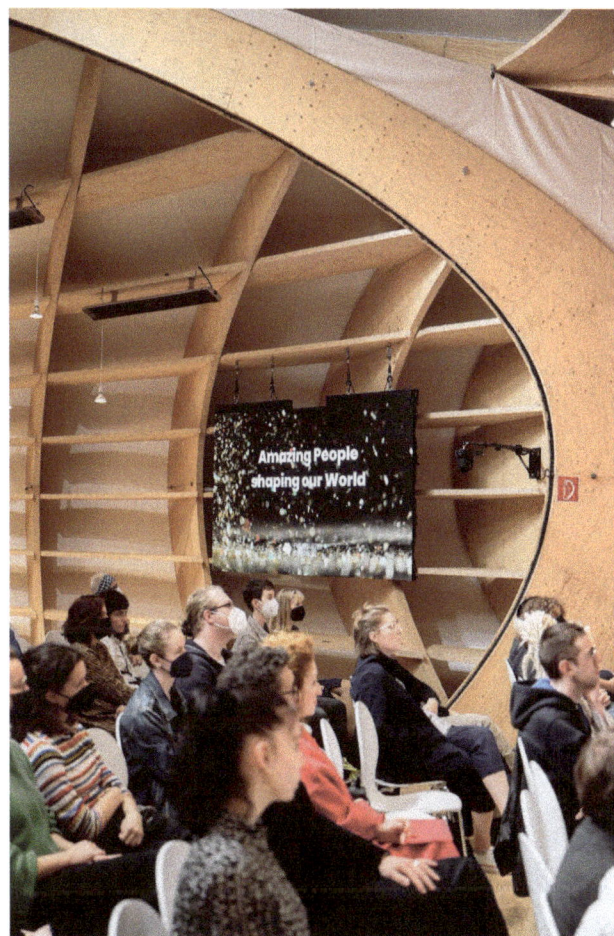

Frankffurter Buchmesse/Domenic Driessen

The "Publishing Perspectives Forum," held on Wednesday and Thursday, offered a lifeline for indie publishers at the fair. The annual forum can be a good place to meet other like-minded authors and publishers and to have your mind blown once or twice before you go home to your creative business. Every publisher has the challenge of making their books visible, and several speakers in the forum emphasized big publishers can pay more for both keywords and social media influencers compared with small, indie publishers. Sound familiar? Once again, there's more to the story.

It's helpful to catch a glimpse of other publishers' creative processes. What shifts your mind into productive overdrive is unique to you and your work, but here are a few mind-blowing moments from this year's forum:

Author and translator, Lawrence Schimel, gave his personal insight on how to work the fair, saying, "You need three Frankfurts" to ink a deal. The first time you attend the Frankfurt Book Fair, people say, "pleased to meet you," he said. The second time, they say, "okay, you're serious," and the third time is when contracts are drawn up.

Rüdiger Wischenbart, founder of Content and Consulting and moderator of the session, called tasks like creating a summary, collecting sample translations, compiling five key selling points per book, and an author interview the "hard, basic homework of publishing."

"You become visible by going out where you can be seen," said Benas Barantas of Book Smugglers Agency. "Make it [your marketing plan] as personal as possible, because the pandemic shows that people need more personal connection. Maybe that's the secret sauce."

The business model for the UK publisher Unbound is a combination of crowdfunding to test a book's potential audience, followed by traditional publishing for the projects that prove themselves. Pointing out that every new social media

Frankffurter Buchmesse/Ingo Hattendorf

platform has gone through a slide from "authentic" to "paid," Unbound encourages readers to have a "more intimate" connection with authors.

Pei-shan Huang is publisher and editor-in-chief of Slowork Publishing in Taiwan. She's also a graphic artist. She silk-screened three hundred copies each of four graphic novels a year, but it wasn't enough content to grow a big audience. Readers in Taiwan were unfamiliar with the graphic novel genre. "We need more publishers," Huang said.

How can readers find your work in 2022? These small publishers highlighted consistency, the "hard, basic work" of publishing, "going out where you can be seen," staying true to your authentic vision, and—most surprising at the book Olympics, considering its size—more competition as a way to create more readers in your genre.

FRANKFURT AND SHAKESPEARE

One of the resounding messages of the 2022 fair was that, today, there are more ways than ever to get your work seen.

In 1622, Shakespeare's "First Folio" was introduced at a Frankfurt Book Fair around seven years after the playwright's death. Although famous in English-speaking countries in his own lifetime, the first print publication of his work made him an international "literary legend."

The printing press created a book industry. The pandemic forced publishing to create new networks. In 2020, the Frankfurt Book Fair made more technological leaps, broadcasting from the fairgrounds and creating new tools and a virtual experience. Many publishers and agents reached out in new ways during this time.

In the *Publishing Perspectives Forum*, a senior rights agent reported using contact information from the fair to make the "highest number of rights deals in five years" via Zoom and email. The Frankfurt Rights database (https://frankfurtrights.com) is free to access for rights "Buyers." According to Thomas Minkus, vice president of English Language Markets for the Frankfurt Book Fair, in a seminar for the fair in 2020, this tool was created "to facilitate what we usually do in Frankfurt."

Another example of an innovative network is "Publishers Without Borders," the international group of publishers that became an online community during this time. More information can be found via the organization's Facebook group, PUBLISHERS WITHOUT BORDERS; on Twitter @pwbspeaks; on Clubhouse at PWB; or on LinkedIn at Publishers Without Borders.

FRANKFURT AND FOMO

By now, you might have serious FOMO. "It's all very nice," you may be saying, "but I can't get to the Frankfurt Book Fair." With the size of the event, even attendees can feel like they've missed out on key takeaways. But we've got good news—the Frankfurt Book Fair offers plenty of opportunities to browse at home. This year's highlights can be found on the fair's website: https://buchmesse.de/en/highlights/media-library. You can also visit the Frankfurt Book Fair website under the "Events" tab to find a new opportunity or idea for your indie business. Note the checkbox to search only expired events with recordings.

If the search form paralyzes you or you want more bite-sized insights from the book Olympics, the *Publishing Perspectives* newsletter shares news and articles related to the global publishing industry. It's like *Publishers Weekly*, but for the whole world. Download a free magazine on the organization's website to learn more about the 2022 Frankfurt Book Fair, NFTs, publishing in China, or other topics.

Even if you weren't at this year's fair and have no immediate plans to visit, your work can be part of the worldwide conversation. If the fair's history is any proof, keep on keeping on with the hard, basic work of publishing, use the available technology, and maybe the Frankfurt Book Fair will remember your books in the year 2422. It worked for the bard!

Laurel Decher

Frankffurter Buchmesse/Zino Peterek

Mark Dawson's Not-So-Secret Formula

THE ESTABLISHED INDIE REFLECTS ON HIS DECISION TO STEER OTHER WRITERS TOWARD SUCCESS

Seven years ago, Mark Dawson told the world in detail how he got his Thriller novels into the hands of hundreds of thousands of readers. His story came in the form of the inaugural Self Publishing Formula online advertising programs, and if you were a member of the Facebook Group or enrolled in one of the courses at the time, you had a front-row seat to hear an indie superstar's modus operandi.

Mark has shared his story plenty of times since then, at conferences, in courses, and with indie authors around the world, in every stage of the publishing journey. But why? Wouldn't sharing these secrets make his future success harder as more authors employed the same techniques?

It was a serious consideration back in 2015.

Mark went from frustrated traditionally published author to clumsy and unsuccessful self-published author to international success story in just a few short years. He learned at the feet of giants such as bestselling author Hugh C. Howey and adapted their techniques into a system that thousands of indie authors have used since.

At the center of his methodology is a combination of Facebook ads and a well-demonstrated, dependable mailing list strategy. But Mark realized early on that he had to nail the entire process to succeed. He'd set

his books' prices low, typically $3.99 or $4.99, so there was no room for "leaks" in the flow, he says. Eventually, he found a process that worked—but as time went on, he became frustrated watching other talented writers languish with few or no sales in their own businesses. That was the prompt to start sharing, he says.

"I used to spend a lot of time in the indie online forums," Mark says. "I remember seeing a few success stories, but they were outnumbered by authors who simply didn't know where to start, or worse, they were pouring money into advertising, but nothing else about their setup was right."

So, in 2015, he founded the Self Publishing Formula. "It's not the best name, on reflection, but we're stuck with it," he says. "There is no single formula. It's better described using the adage coined by the British Cycling Team after their rise to global dominance: 'the accumulation of marginal gains.'"

Mark understood what needed to be in place to succeed. He'd cracked the code of paid ads, though he admits he lost thousands of dollars while he learned before the needle started to rise.

"Creating SPF [Self Publishing Formula] was a huge task," he says. "At its core, I wanted to offer professional, highly produced online courses that would take authors of all experience levels

through the process of building a winning platform. I knew I couldn't do it on my own, so I called two former colleagues from my film classification days, James Blatch and John Dyer. They immediately said yes, and SPF was born over a coffee at the BFI Cinema in Southbank."

In the years since, Blatch has become well known in indie circles in his own right, thanks to his role as the co-host of SPF's weekly podcast, the Self Publishing Show. In 2016, he began writing his own novel, and listeners have followed along with every bump in the road since then. Today, Blatch has two novels published, both selling well, and a third in the pipeline. "In many ways, James is the perfect example of what I wanted to achieve," Mark says. "He started with nothing, not even a completed manuscript. Today, he makes a regular profit from his two Thrillers in a niche sub-genre. He's got to that point by following the courses he himself helped to create."

Blatch is far from alone in his success, and Mark's decision to share his hard-won wisdom with other authors has certainly

had a ripple effect on the indie author community at large. But has it cost Mark sales in exchange?

"Probably," he admits. "I think it's quite likely that I could have made hay for a little longer while others caught up. But that's not something that bothers me. And while several thousand authors have followed my methods in detail, it's still a drop in the ocean.

"The sad truth is the vast majority will not engage with the marketing side of publishing," he continues. "They'll write a few books, become frustrated with lack of success, and most likely give up. I'm not talking about the authors we interact with in the groups. I'm talking about those who don't even get that far. The fact that someone is reading *Indie Author Magazine* or listening to the Self Publishing Show immediately elevates them above the masses. You are much more likely to succeed just by immersing yourself in the online world of indie authors."

For its part, the Self Publishing Formula offers authors plenty of opportunity for such immersion in the community. Its Facebook group is host to a thriving community of indies. The Self Publishing Show podcast has become a renowned resource for writers, with guests from every corner of the industry. "We've released more than 350 episodes now—that's nearly seven years," Mark says. "I won't say it's an easy task. It's not. James in particular has to carry out an interview each week, and we have a small army in the background making sure we get a fresh episode out every Friday. But it's become a bit of an institution in the indie world. We don't restrict ourselves to marketing either—the show is a place where we talk as much about craft as we do business. We also feature traditionally published authors and industry figures from all areas. It's been a fascinating experience. We've had a front-row seat as publishing changes forever."

And beyond the Facebook Group, the Self Publishing Show, and Mark's own ads courses, the group also boasts two acclaimed premium courses, Advertising for Authors and Launchpad.

"Launchpad, as the name suggests, is the starting point," Mark says. "Split across ten modules, it's the largest course we offer, including a comprehensive technical library for those tricky processes we all need to master. The course is designed to take an author from typing the words 'The End' to making a steady income from book sales. Ads for Authors is the next step. To continue the space analogy from Launchpad, this is the fuel that you need to really lift off."

Both courses are open for enrollment at specific times of the year, he says. "We like to onboard students in batches. As an organization, we spend as much time making sure authors get value from the courses as we do creating them."

Besides the two courses, the Self Publishing Formula also has three "evergreen" options that are permanently available. These cover the craft side of the industry, something Mark himself stays away from.

"I've never felt comfortable teaching the craft side of writing," Mark admits. "I don't analyze my writing to the point where I understand how or why it works. But others do, and we are very lucky to have Suzy K. Quinn as the author of our writing course, 'How to Write a Bestseller.' In addition we have Stuart Bache, who has worked on designs for Stephen King and John Le Carré, presenting 'Cover Design for Authors.' Finally, we have Jennie Nash—somebody with immense industry experience as an editor—and 'How to Revise Your Book.' Combined, these three courses take an author from staring at a blank page all the way to having a polished manuscript and a killer publishing package. By then they're ready to embark on the commercial side of their business, which is where I step in."

From where he started in 2015, Mark's success—and his status—have undoubtedly blossomed, and if the self-publishing industry's own growth is anything to go on, there's little sign of it slowing down. Any sign of the seven-year itch?

"Absolutely not," Mark says. "The indie world is thriving, and we are too. And if there's ever a moment when I think it's all a bit much, I visit our testimonials page and listen to the many authors we've interviewed about the success our courses have given them—writers like Shayne Silvers, who unbeknown to his wife had to cash in their life savings as a last-ditch attempt to invest in his author career. Now he's a millionaire and a writer adored by his many fans. There's also the amazing Lucy Score, sacked from her job when they discovered she was writing Steamy Romance on the side. It was the investment in Ads for Authors that saw her and her partner Tim turn her books into Amazon number 1 bestsellers. And there are plenty more, including authors who make enough to pay their mortgage each month or can quit the nine-to-five job they hate. That's all the motivation I need to continue SPF."

Design like a Pro for free

👑 Try Canva Pro today

Canva

https://writelink.to/canva

Q&A: Indie Author Experts Reflect on Industry Growth and Where We're Headed in 2023

For the indie author community, 2022 has undoubtedly been a year for the books. In February, Draft2Digital announced the acquisition of Smashwords, bringing two of the largest independent distributors of self-published books together under one name. Less than a month later, Sci-Fi and Fantasy author Brandon Sanderson made history with a Kickstarter project that earned more than forty-one million dollars over the course of the campaign. Thanks to the continued growth of reading communities on Instagram, Twitter, and TikTok, countless indie authors have seen their books top bestseller charts thanks to social media. And if the record-setting vendor presence at November's 20Books Vegas conference is any indication, authors this year have more platforms, tools, and technology available to help grow their businesses than ever before.

Now, as we set our sights on the new year, seasoned indie authors are offering their thoughts on what self-published authors can look forward to in 2023. For Draft2Digital Director of Marketing and Public Relations Kevin Tumlinson and Joanna Penn of The Creative Penn podcast, that means new opportunities in the world of AI tools, whereas for USA TODAY bestselling author Russell Nohelty, that means more chances for authors to explore marketing and distribution models that work best for their businesses.

Note: Responses have been edited for length and clarity.

IAM

WHAT ARE THE MOST IMPORTANT DEVELOPMENTS THAT HAVE COME ABOUT FOR INDIE AUTHORS THIS YEAR?

KEVIN Tumlinson

I think the biggest thing to come out in 2022 for the indie author community is the acquisition of Smashwords by Draft2Digital. … It's opening up a lot of doors for indie authors in terms of increasing their reach, increasing the number of storefronts that can hit but also empowering them by giving them their own store, basically. It's the indie author sales platform where they get a bigger royalty than they get from any other retailer.

JOANNA Penn

I don't think most authors have adopted AI tools in terms of their creative process as of yet, but authors have been using AI for years. What's new this year is generative AI, and generative AI is using AI tools as part of the creative process. I'm an absolute fan of using AI, but none of it is just press a button and output a finished novel or a finished book cover. It can only deliver to a creative vision. That's the change in 2022—the move from using AI for our publishing and marketing into using AI for the generative sense.

RUSSELL Nohelty

I've basically been wide my whole career, and talking to people about being wide before, you would think that I had three heads or told them I was going to shoot a baby into the sun. And as time's gone on, it's slowly chipped away at that. But I think this year was a seismic shift. I was at a convention, and someone asked how many people have considered going wide, and 70 percent of the hands went up. I was shocked because in this crowd, if it's not working for them, Kindle Unlimited can't possibly be working for anyone.

IAM

WHAT CHALLENGES DO INDIE AUTHORS FACE?

KEVIN Tumlinson

Amazon has always been the go-to, number one place for people to buy e-books for the indie author community … but the shifts in the way Amazon does things, that is kind of having detrimental effects on the industry and the community. We have no insight into what's happening or how things work, but we do know when something has changed because we will see things like our sales drop or our promotions disappear, and there seems to be no internal promotion. It would help the community a great deal if people stopped doing exclusivity within Amazon because it's basically locked up the industry a bit.

JOANNA Penn

Visibility is a challenge, but to be fair, it's always been a challenge. My recommendation … is to build an email list. Technology is still a really powerful thing, and if you own your list, and you own your website and you own your intellectual property assets, you can continue to make a living or earn money or reach readers, whatever your definition of success is, regardless of the change. Everything changes, and you have to keep reinventing yourself, but the email list has really stood the test of time.

RUSSELL Nohelty

I think the biggest challenge is people trying to figure out how they can create an ecosystem for themselves that works for them. It does take a lot of effort to build the marketing and the author ecosystem. The challenge is making that transition is super hard—to go from thinking, "I'm an author who just turns on ads when I do a launch, and money comes out the other end" to "Oh, I have to be very strategic" is very tough. But every other creative industry, from movies to films to television to fine art, has made that transition. And I think that they're all better for it.

IAM

WHAT DO YOU HOPE TO SEE CHANGE?

KEVIN Tumlinson

I think every author should be aiming for wide distribution over exclusivity with Amazon or anyone else. They lure you in with what seems like easy money, and then you're kind of stuck because you've been spending all your energy and time marketing to a specific segment of a specific audience. Everyone who I've ever met wanted their books to be available worldwide to as many people as possible. That's just not going to happen. Amazon only has a limited market share worldwide.

JOANNA Penn

I hope that there's more of an empowerment in the community to connect directly with readers. What I think will happen in 2023 is, finally, authors are going to start selling direct more. What we've seen this year in 2022 is a realization that the existing digital abundance model is starting to break and that the best way for authors to make money is to go direct to readers. They'll be even less visible because it will all be direct, but most independent authors, I think, are more interested in making a living and connecting with readers.

RUSSELL Nohelty

Most authors who are unsuccessful believe their books are bad. They believe there is some problem with their book that prevents it from being successful. And that is not an untrue statement all the time. But so often we find authors who write great books, but they're trying to fit a square peg in a round hole. Their decision to put their books in Kindle Unlimited or however they're choosing to market their books is where the fault is, especially if you have a good cover, a good blurb, a good look inside, your formatting is good, you're hiring an editor, you're doing all of those actions.

WHAT ARE YOU LOOKING FORWARD TO FOR THE INDUSTRY IN 2023?

KEVIN Tumlinson

AI is going to be a tremendous tool for indie authors. What I see happening on the AI front is authors are going to have … the ability to have a competitive edge without increasing their overhead and without having to break their budget. These things are not competing with the traditional creators in that field. Instead, it's creating a whole new market.

JOANNA Penn

What I hope to see in 2023 is more authors adopting the use of these creative tools as part of their creation process. I think what's really important to emphasize is that this augments our creativity, and it enhances and, I believe, amplifies our creative vision. What I fully expect is more authors will be using these tools, but the language will change so they might not realize they're using a lot of this emerging technology.

RUSSELL Nohelty

What I am excited for in 2023 and 2024 and beyond is people taking control of their authorship and saying, "My book is objectively good. It reads well, it has a good cover, has a good blurb. It has a good look inside; the formatting is good." I'm hoping that we're going to come to a point where people say enough is enough; I'm going to spend time figuring out what works for me. Maybe this series goes wide. Maybe this series I do on Kickstarter. Maybe this series becomes a serialized book. All of these things sort of allow you to build multiple income streams and be less reliant on any one thing to succeed.

IAM

WHAT SHOULD NEW AUTHORS KNOW AHEAD OF THE NEW YEAR?

KEVIN Tumlinson

Don't be afraid to try things; don't be afraid to experiment. Don't limit yourself based on what you think the industry is. Go out and find that segment of the market that appeals to you the most, and if it doesn't exist, write the book anyway and see if you can invent it. This is a very exciting time for indie publishing. We've never had so many resources and so many opportunities. It's just going to keep getting better.

JOANNA Penn

The sort of question for new writers is how are you going to write and how are you going to reach readers? … There are so many options, but the main thing is to find what works for you and your book. … Another tip is to be very careful what contracts you sign, regardless of whether those contracts are with independent companies or traditional publishers because a lot of these contracts will stop you from making the most of the possibilities in the future.

RUSSELL Nohelty

If you're willing to build better habits and take longer to grow and learn more profitable marketing tactics, in the long run, you'll be better off for it. We always talk about Kickstarter and Patreon and wide platforms and direct sales and all of these things. They're not as easy as putting a book on Kindle Unlimited; it takes uploading more places, figuring out what works for you, trying fiction apps, and all the other things that work. But once you develop the system that works for you, you develop those good marketing habits at the beginning, then the long term becomes easier for you.

IAM

WHAT DO YOU ENJOY ABOUT BEING PART OF THE INDIE AUTHOR COMMUNITY?

KEVIN Tumlinson

It's probably the most supportive community I've ever been a part of. Everyone's willing to share what they know, everyone's willing to help out. It's a very empowering community.

JOANNA Penn

It's the focus on creative independence that I value. Creative and financial independence is really what we're about, so being part of that is exciting because there's always something new to learn. Being part of the community keeps pushing me.

RUSSELL Nohelty

Indie authors are so supportive in a way that most entrepreneurs are not. Whenever I go into an author community, they're all so excited about story and new books that are coming out, whether it's theirs or other people's. I find that so comforting. Coming from a world of other entrepreneurs where it's more like, "How can I or my group of friends dominate everything else?" to go be in a community where everyone is trying to pull everyone up is incredible.

Kristin Rodin and Nicole Schroeder

7 Steps to Your Perfect Five-Year Publishing Plan

It's almost the end of another year and time once more for setting intentions for the future. But don't reach for a soapbox about New Year's resolutions or dust off your schemes for world domination just yet. However well you think these goals work in your personal life, the new year can also be the perfect opportunity to map out a path for your author business over the next five years.

We can hear the groans now. Drawing up a five-year plan sounds boring, business-like, and not at all creative. But if you want to treat your author career like a business, well, it's a necessity. Proper planning, even if it's kept basic at the start, is a must for selecting the right goals and for seeing them realized.

A five-year plan is simply a map to get you from where you started to where you want to be. For new authors, the first year of your plan might entail the more mundane process of setting up your author business, including choosing a company structure, such as an LLC or DBA. It might include designing a logo, planning your website, setting up social media, or researching your chosen genre or genres. Your plan is likely to change as you come across things you didn't even know to consider and as you learn how you work as an author, how fast you write, and what's realistic for you. For experienced authors, creating a five-year plan is more likely to be about moving yourself up to the next level. You'll be well past the basics and on to building your author brand, building your team, growing your audience, and increasing your monthly and yearly income. Your plan is more likely to include tasks such as arranging for translations or audiobooks, licensing, considering new genres, building your mailing list, running paid ads, creating additional streams of income, or organizing movie or TV deals.

Still, no matter where you are in your career, a five-year plan is useful for keeping you on track, keeping you focused on your goals, and preventing overwhelm.

DREAM A LITTLE DREAM

Where do you want to be in five years' time? What do you want to have achieved?

These questions might seem vague, but knowing how you'd answer them is essential as you draft your five-year plan. This is the time to let your imagination go wild. You can plan and be practical later, but for now, enjoy picturing yourself polishing your future awards or moving bespoke furniture into your dream house. Get into the details, and imagine how you'd feel.

Build up a picture of where you'll be in five years, and write it down at the top of your page. This will help you find the target you're aiming for.

Speaking of fun, make your planning an enjoyable process, and one that's unique to you. Although it may sound like something a corporate exec would do—and it is—it doesn't have to be boring. Use stickers, stars, and washi tape to organize your page, or if you'd prefer, type into an online document, lay it out in a spreadsheet, or use organizational software. Monday.com offers a free template on its blog that you can fill out or use as inspiration in formatting your own document: https://monday.com/blog/task-management/5-year-plan-template/. You can also find five-year planners online that include full diaries, calendars, notes, space for sketching, goal worksheets, yearly goal planners. Some are bound books, but if you'd like more customizable options, some offer printable worksheets so you can select what you find most helpful and organize it as you see fit.

Your five-year plan should be as much a source of inspiration as it is organization, so paste in images of the house you want to buy with your royalties or scribble in quotes from authors who've made it to where you want to be. Include rewards at certain milestones for meeting your goals, and remember that in the long term, keeping yourself motivated while working toward your chosen end goal will be just as important as the plan you're crafting now.

CHOOSE YOUR GOALS

When you put together a five-year plan, you need to know your ultimate end goals for year five, but you also need to have goals for each year that lead to achieving your ultimate goals. If you want to hit six figures in year five, for example, you need to understand what activities, tasks, and events will get you there and ensure that these things are in your planner at the right time of each month and year.

Add these milestone goals to your planner to break your objectives into more manageable chunks, as well as to give yourself a way to stay accountable and keep track of your progress.

When you choose your goals, be specific. Include dollar amounts for how much you'd like to earn or the number of titles you'd like to have published. It's far better to say that you want to earn $500,000 a year by year five than it is to say that you want to have more than enough money to pay your bills. The second option is too wooly and unclear, and you won't be able to adequately measure your progress down the road.

3 BUILD AROUND EXISTING PLANS

Before you break down the steps you'll need to make toward your objective each year, consider your current commitments. Add any conferences, book signings, speaker opportunities, courses that you'll be taking, and/or firm book release dates and deadlines. If you've already booked any vacations, include those too.

Once existing plans are in, it's easier to work out what happens on the run up to each event or release. It'll also make it easier to understand your availability to work on additional projects throughout each year and the steps you're already taking toward your larger goals.

4 PLAN YOUR BOOK PUBLISHING SCHEDULE

It may be tempting to fill your year with tasks and to-dos, but be honest when setting deadlines about how fast you finish a book and how many books you're likely to publish in one year. Experienced authors are likely to have this down, but newer authors may not know how long they need to write a book. If you're new, start with a very flexible plan that you can adjust as you learn, and try not to overcommit yourself. It's better to only plan two books for this year and beat your goal than it is to plan ten and only manage five.

Your plan is there to help you meet your goals, and no one else has to know what it says. Other authors are not your competition, so focus on your goals and priorities, and make sure they're reasonable for your writing speed. The alternative won't help you reach your goals any faster and could in fact work against you over time, affecting your mental health and/or leading to burnout.

5 WORK BACKWARD

Once you have your major events and releases written for the next five years, it's easier to look at each one and work backward on your plan to figure out where you need to start. Break each target into small, manageable tasks that you can complete step by step.

Something like "write book" won't help you understand the amount of work you need to accomplish or where to start, but steps like "complete outline," "update bio," "write blurb," and "add new preorder" are easier to approach and will keep you from feeling overwhelmed. Add these onto your calendar in whichever order works for you, ensuring you've left enough time to get everything done.

As you fill out your schedule, include time for beta readers, the various stages of editing, ARC readers and reviews, and marketing, and keep in mind that you may need to adjust your schedule at a later date based on things like your editor's availability. It might be best to plan in pencil first so you can erase or reorganize your schedule closer to the date.

ALLOW FOR "YOU TIME"

No author can write or work on publishing-related tasks seven days a week, 365 days a year. You can try, but you will inevitably write yourself toward burnout.

As tempting as it is to fill your schedule to the brim and imagine how much you could accomplish, it's just as important to schedule times for rest throughout the year. Consider that you're going to want vacation time during the next five years, and there are likely to be significant personal events, such as family weddings or big birthdays, that you'll want to attend.

Maybe you want to take more time writing your books so you can have evenings and weekends free, if you're a full-time author. Maybe you know you need a week to recover when you've finished your latest book, or even a month. Think about what you need to work at your best, and plan to provide yourself with that.

Your plan should help your writing fit in with your life while still getting everything done and not allow it to take over entirely.

REMAIN FLEXIBLE

In any long-term schedule, you'll need to allow for some wiggle room. Life happens. Your schedule might need to be adjusted if you or a family member get sick. You might find you have free time suddenly if a book falls through or gets pushed back, or you might have the perfect opportunity fall into your lap two years down the road—something you never would've thought to plan for, yet something you just can't turn down.

Don't make your schedule air-tight. Allow yourself some breathing room in between books, just in case. Plan a little extra time to meet your deadlines so you don't have to push yourself harder than you like to work.

As you build out your schedule, add your must-do book projects first. You can then add a couple of extras toward the end of the year that would be nice to work on if you have the time. This gives you the freedom to drop the optional projects if something unexpected comes up without causing a problem or feeling guilty for not completing everything the way you'd intended.

Finally, don't stress if you aren't able to stick completely to your plan. Your schedule shouldn't be a rigid guilt-trip of a document, glowering at you from the shelf and sighing in disgust every hour it isn't touched. It's meant to be a genuinely helpful, flexible outline that works for you and with you in growing your business.

Adjust if needed, and don't worry about needing to alter your course of action. Your plan is a guide toward your bigger goals each year, but there's no right path for how to reach them. As long as you continue making progress, you'll find that, no matter how long it takes, hitting your goals will push you to aim even higher.

No one can know for sure where they'll be in the next five years. But with a well-considered plan in hand, you'll already be one step closer to hitting your goals and building a successful author career that works for you.

Gill Fernley

Ulysses

A 'JUST WRITE' APP FOR AUTHORS

I've written at least one book with darned near every major—and most of the minor—writing apps out there on the market: Google Docs, Microsoft Word, 4theWords, Atticus, Scrivener, Novlr, Pages. I've even written a book in Vellum before. Trying out new writing software has become something of a hobby of mine over the years.

But the app I keep coming back to is called Ulysses.

Ulysses bills itself as "The Ultimate Writing App for Mac, iPad and iPhone." They may actually be on point with that description, but I'll let you judge for yourself. That one-liner also encapsulates the sole drawback to using Ulysses: It's for Apple devices only. There's no Android or Windows version, and I don't believe there are plans to make one.

That said, for Apple device users, it can be a reliable and user-friendly piece of software. I'm using it to write this article, in fact. And of course I've written many novels in Ulysses as well. With a flexible and extensible tree structure for files, a system that allows users to search by keyword so you can find just the right file, a "Markdown"-based writing experience so one's fingers never leave the keys, and the most reliable cross-device file syncing I've ever seen in a writing app, Ulysses certainly stands out among the crowd.

WHAT MAKES ULYSSES DIFFERENT?

Ulysses is built around a tree-style file structure, similar to Scrivener. This is one of the things I like best about the app. It allows me to set up a category for a series of books, then a subcategory for each book, and individual pages within the subcategory for each chapter. At a glance, I have all of my books there, easy to find and look through. There's no note board like Scrivener has, but you can reorder chapters with little difficulty.

Pro Tip: I use the tree file structure to organize my books as well. Each file is a chapter, and each chapter is nested inside a group of files for a novel. Each novel is then nested inside another group for that series of novels. This lets me quickly find specific chapters from books I wrote years ago with just a few clicks.

You can also assign keywords to files, allowing you to search for just the right scene or chapter based on its tag. For example, you can assign character keywords to note which chapter files feature which characters or to divide chapters by viewpoints.

Ulysses works on all Apple devices and stores its data in iCloud by default, though you can also have it back up via Dropbox. I've left it on iCloud, myself, though I export finished works to Dropbox for long-term storage. The synchronization

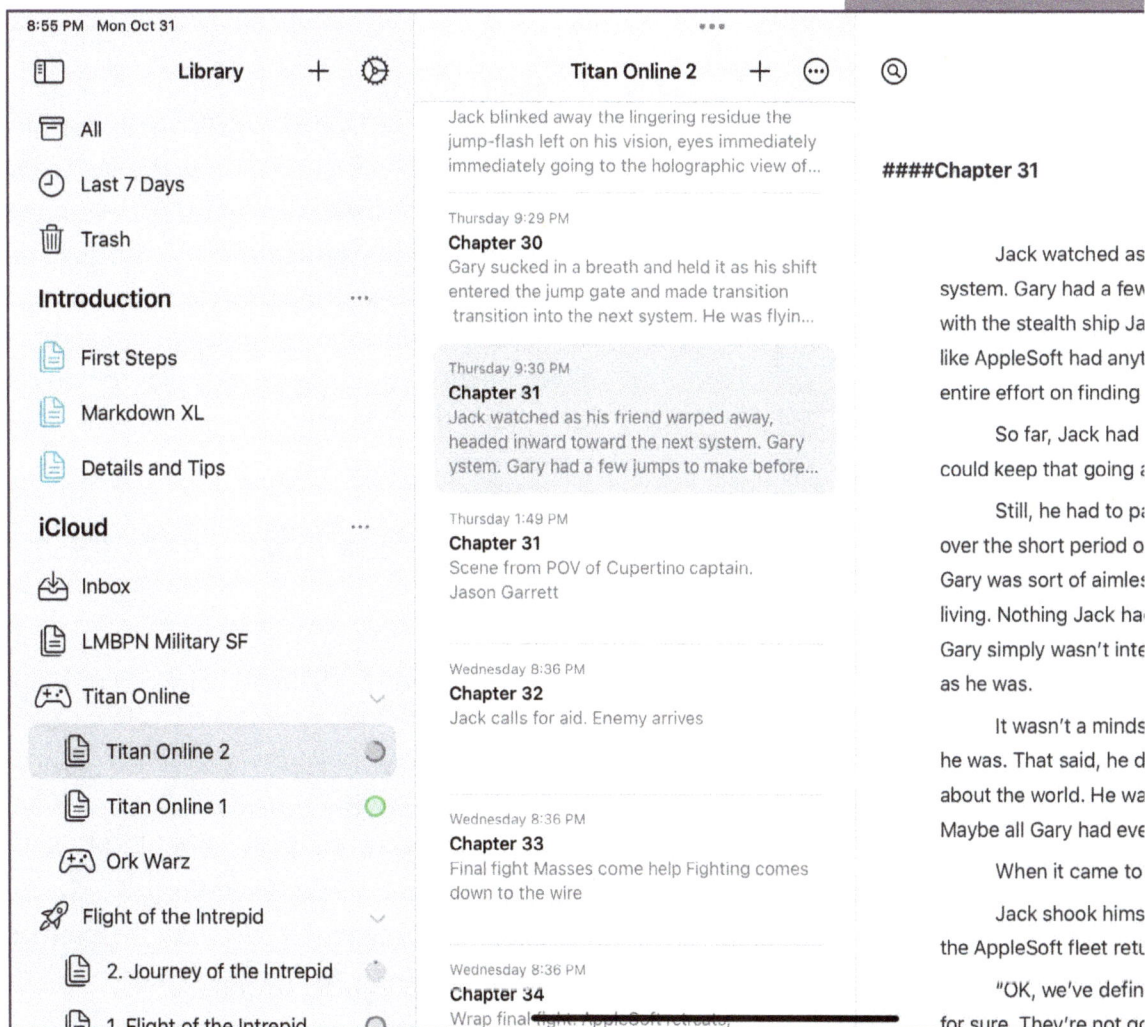

across devices is peerless. For me, this is exceptionally important because I'm often working on my iPad and sometimes even on my iPhone. The files transfer fluidly and almost instantly between all internet-connected Apple devices, and Ulysses works like a dream on iPads and iPhones, as well as Macs.

Formatting documents in Ulysses can be a bit of a learning curve thanks to its feature called "Markdown." Markdown is a way of formatting your text in-line by using visible characters. For example, if I want to show something in italics, I type an asterisk before and after the word. If I want it in bold, I put two asterisks before and two after the bolded section. There are several Markdown elements, including things for quotes, headers, code blocks, and more. Ulysses saves the files in Markdown, but when you export the compiled work, the app automatically changes the Markdown shortcuts into formatting. More advanced formatting features are also available at the time of export, including options to design your own specialized export formatting.

For many writers, this feels more seamless. I don't have to remove my fingers from the keyboard to select text and bold it, for example. I don't even have to move my hands to hit Command+B. I can just hit a couple of asterisks and get the same effect. It's not a huge time saver, but it does have an impact. And it takes a wee bit of getting used to if you haven't played with Markdown before, but don't worry; once you get the hang of it, the feature can be super easy.

OTHER COOL FEATURES?

Ulysses has a "just right" export system, midway between Microsoft Word's fairly bland options and Scrivener's incredibly complex setup. Ulysses gives users powerful options but also allows for nearly one-click exports for simple documents.

Ulysses exports in PDF, EPUB, HTML, DOCX, RTF, TXT, and a few other formats. Because it was designed for bloggers, it also can be connected—and export directly—to Wordpress, Ghost, or Medium blogs.

Close   Rich Text   ⬆

HTML

Ulysses has an awesome export   o easy to use. Click Export and
you'll be asked what format you   ePub   ML, DOCX, RTF, TXT, and a few
other formats. Because it was de   it also can be connected to—
and export directly to—Wordpres   PDF

There's also a built-in proofreadi   ammar and spelling needs. It
doesn't have all the bells and wh   DOCX   but it's comparable with the
checks in Word, for example.

With a few clicks I can go into an   s and goals. These can be
characters, words, sentences, pa   Plain Text   tracks how close I am to my
goal with a visual image of a fillir   yourself.

Personally, I write in Ulysses witt   ✓ Rich Text   aid out on the left side of my
screen. But if you prefer a distrac   can do that, too! You can easily
make the side-bar vanish and tur   eady for your work.
                                           Markdown
What's the cost?
                                           TextPack

Ulysses is a software-as-a-servic   n ongoing subscription fee to
keep it active. I confess that whe   Publishing   ystem, I was not a happy
camper. I generally don't like SA,   nce and then not getting
charged again. I dropped Ulysses and went off to try a bunch of other apps.

And...I came back to Ulysses, because in spite of the annual fee, it's simply the best app I've found to
do my work. For me, Ulysses just rocks.

The cost is $39.99 a year; students can get a slightly reduced rate of $11.99 for six months, and there's
a free trial to give it a shot before you buy.

In return, the developers are actually pushing hard to continue work on the program. For example, when
the M1 machines first came out and a lot of software was having issues running on it, Ulysses came out
with a patch immediately and my work wasn't interrupted by even a single day of bugs. Likewise, in all
the years I've used Ulysses I've never had issues making it work with a new operating system update.
The devs are always enough ahead of Apple's operating system releases that it's always a bug-free
experience.

If that's the results of users spending forty bucks a year for the app? I guess I can live with that.

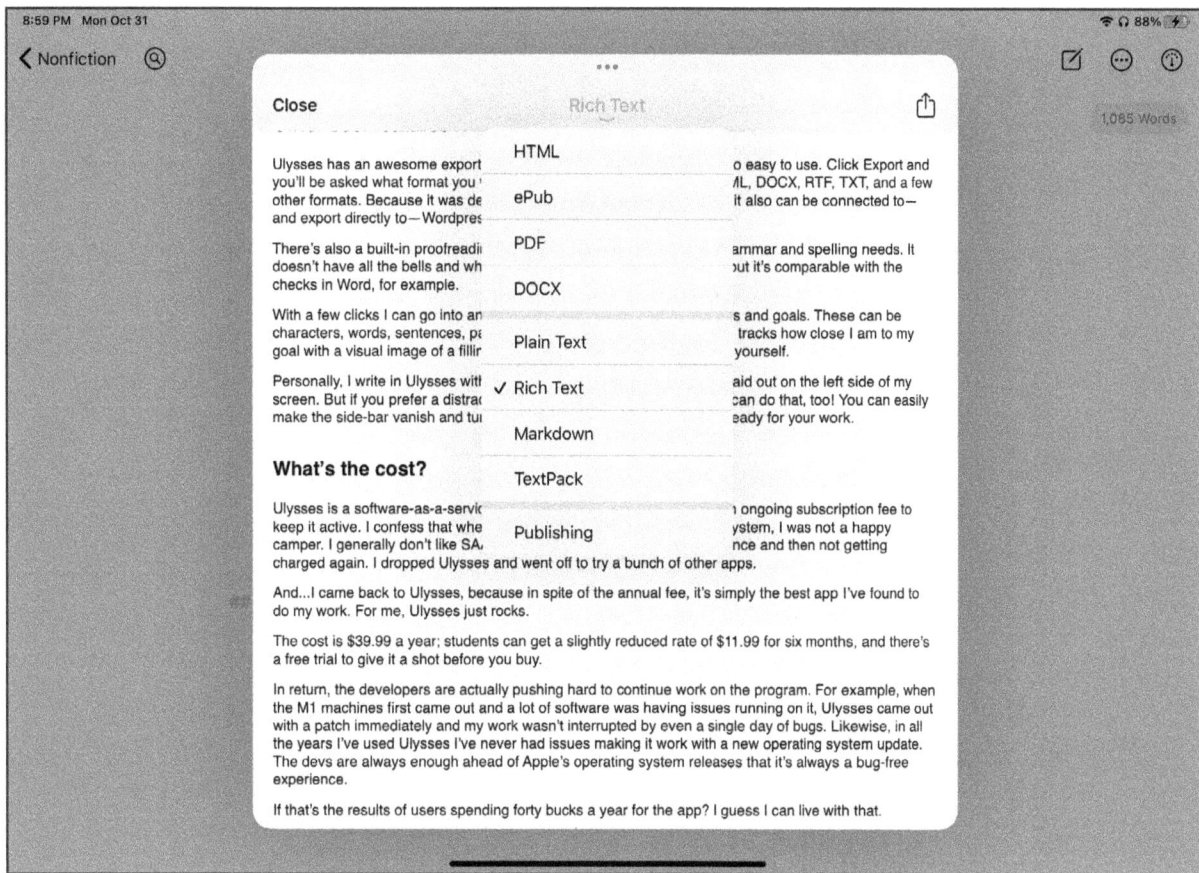

On the writing side, the built-in proofreading function can cover all your basic grammar and spelling needs. It doesn't have all the bells and whistles of something like ProWritingAid, but it's comparable with the checks in Microsoft Word, for example. You can also set deadlines for yourself. With a few clicks, I can go into any file or collection of files and set targets and goals. These can be characters, words, sentences, paragraphs, or even pages. Ulysses then tracks how close I am to my goal with a visual image of a filling circle.

Personally, I write in Ulysses with the sidebar showing all my chapters laid out on the left side of my screen. But if you prefer a distraction-free writing environment, Ulysses can do that too. You can easily make the sidebar vanish and turn the entire screen into a blank page, ready for your work.

WHAT'S THE COST?

Ulysses is a software-as-a-service (SAAS) application; that is, there's an ongoing subscription fee to keep it active. I confess that when the developers first switched to this system in 2017, I was not a happy camper. I generally don't like SAAS applications. I much prefer paying once and not being charged again. I dropped Ulysses and went off to try a bunch of other apps.

Yet I came back to Ulysses because, in spite of the annual fee, it's simply the best app I've found to do my work. The powerful synchronization between devices, simple but flexible export system, and terrific file organization structure make this my tool of choice.

Pro Tip: Subscribers can suggest new features they'd like to see implemented, and the development team is extremely responsive toward user requests. This lets us as users help steer the course of future development for Ulysses.

A subscription costs $5.99 a month or $39.99 a year; students can get a slightly reduced rate of $11.99 for six months, and there's a fourteen-day free trial to give it a shot before you buy.

In return, the developers are actually pushing hard to continue work on the program. For example, when the M1 machines first came out, Ulysses came out with a patch immediately, and my work wasn't interrupted by even a single day of bugs. Likewise, in all the years I've used Ulysses, I've never had issues making it work with a new operating system update. The developers stay enough ahead of Apple's operating system releases that it's generally a bug-free experience.

If that's the results of users spending forty bucks a year for the app? I figure I'm getting my money's worth.

Give it a shot!

A writer's chosen tool is something that's incredibly personal, and no app is going to be perfect for everyone. But this one is particularly good, and I recommend giving it a test run to see if you like it. With the program's free trial, there's really nothing to lose but a little time, so pick up your iPad or Mac, download Ulysses, and give it a spin. In my experience, it's one of the finest writing apps available today.

Kevin McLaughlin

AUTHOR·TECH·SUMMIT

January 18-23, 2023

AuthorTechSummit.com

Go direct to
your readers
via your own
website.

We'll show
you how.

Sign up for
ATS January
2023.

Making the List

A MULTI-TIME BESTSELLER RECOUNTS HER ROAD TO THE TOP

Achieving bestseller status is a dream many indie authors feel inspired to pursue. Gaining a bestseller title from prestigious publications such as Wall Street Journal or USA TODAY not only gives an author an accolade for their title, but it can also change the path of their career. However, the process of earning the title can be more demanding—and more costly—than you might expect. To gain perspective on just what a list-making run entails, it helps to walk in the shoes of someone who has done it many times before.

Renee Rose is a multi-time USA TODAY bestselling author and the author of the new release Write To Riches: 7 Practical Steps to Manifesting Abundance from Your Books. Her past five co-authored titles made the USA TODAY Bestsellers list, and she's recently had a list hit with a solo title.

Rose's latest new release made the USA TODAY list without a marketing push, accumulating four thousand auto buys on the first day. Rose began her bestseller career making the USA TODAY list with multi-author anthologies, climbing her way up a self-described ladder of success in order to make the list on her own.

"The first five or six times were anthology list runs. The first time was to get my letters [make a bestseller list], and the other anthology runs were to help other people get theirs," Rose says. She'd recommend the path to other authors, though it does come with some risk. "Ninety-nine-cent anthology runs are a great way to start because you can split the cost with other authors, and we always made the money back. We've made the list with as little as three thousand dollars; however, we also missed it with three thousand."

Once she had several anthology titles under her belt, Rose focused on building her brand by making a list with her co-author, without enticing readers with a discounted book.

"Another bar to climb was hitting the list on a full-price book. My co-author and I spent big, more than a thousand dollars a day in Facebook ads, but we didn't need to bring that nervous energy," Rose notes. "We had a frantic energy to it, which I don't think helps—thinking, 'Oh my god, we've got to hit now, and we've got to spend more.' When you bring that energy to it, you're not embodying a bestseller. You're muscling into the energy and forcing it to come."

Rose insists that being in the right frame of mind and having a positive attitude is far more important to any sale than any marketing campaign or promotions could be.

"You can't bring in a fearful energy that you're not good enough and that you're not going to make it. The one book we did a USAT [USA TODAY] run on that didn't hit had that negativity," she says. "Believe in your books, because if you believe in your books, you'll be willing to invest the money and take the risk. You don't want to have the thought, 'I want to hide in the closet and hope I make the list.' If you believe in your book, you'll act accordingly, and when you believe, others will too. The readers will pick up on the energy you're putting out."

Rose notes that her experiences going for a solo title USA TODAY run was different than making a run with a group of authors or even with her co-author. She states that her success came not from a big advertising spend but a change in mindset.

"The first time I had a BookBub for a solo title, the sale wasn't going well, so I pulled back on spending and doubled down on love," she says. "I checked in with my book and asked what it wanted, and the book said, 'I want you to already believe I'm a bestseller.' I was holding back my love, thinking that the book might not be good enough to hit a list. But then I opened up and told the book, 'You're amazing the way you are. I love you and appreciate you, and I'd like you to hit the list.' That's when I made the list with four thousand sales."

The feelings you have around your book and your sale, however, are what Rose emphasizes are most important.

"Ask your book what it needs to hit the list. If it says nothing, to sit back and believe, then do it. If it tells you to book newsletter swaps and post every day, it might need some help. And don't book promotions with that sick feeling of, 'Oh, this is a lot of money to spend.' That'll weigh you down. You could push hard on one release and sit back on the rest," Rose says. "Alternate action; sometimes you have to push big, and sometimes you coast. It's that inner knowing. Trying energy is different than bringing in money energy. You have to be all in."

For practical advice, Rose says that paying attention to multiple areas helps with the longevity of a list-making run. "Book every promotion you can. I've given that advice so many times, and no one takes it. Book promotions you don't even think will work, and make sure to push every platform equally."

Mental health should also be a priority during a list-making run, according to Rose. Take time for self-care and self-love, and know that what you're offering to readers has value and is important to the world. Thinking of yourself and your book as inadequate will only cause the sale to struggle.

"Be an invitation instead of yanking readers in," Rose says. "You can always feel the desperation in a push—a hunger, but not in a good way. Reverse the flow and pull the success in. Be in a state of receiving love from readers instead of a state of giving something to the world that readers don't want."

Rose doesn't believe in gatekeeping; that is, she doesn't believe authors should gatekeep themselves or others when it comes to making a list. She believes every way to earn a USA TODAY title is valid, no matter if it's with a solo author title or in a group anthology. Instead, she encourages authors to believe in themselves and to remove the self-imposed hurdles we are all apt to put on ourselves.

"A short story can hit the USAT [USA TODAY] list just like a full-length novel can," Rose says. "You should be just as proud as making the list with a multi-author anthology as you are a solo title. They're all equal."

This is the second and final story in a series of articles exploring techniques for reaching bestseller status as a self-published author.

Megan Linski-Fox

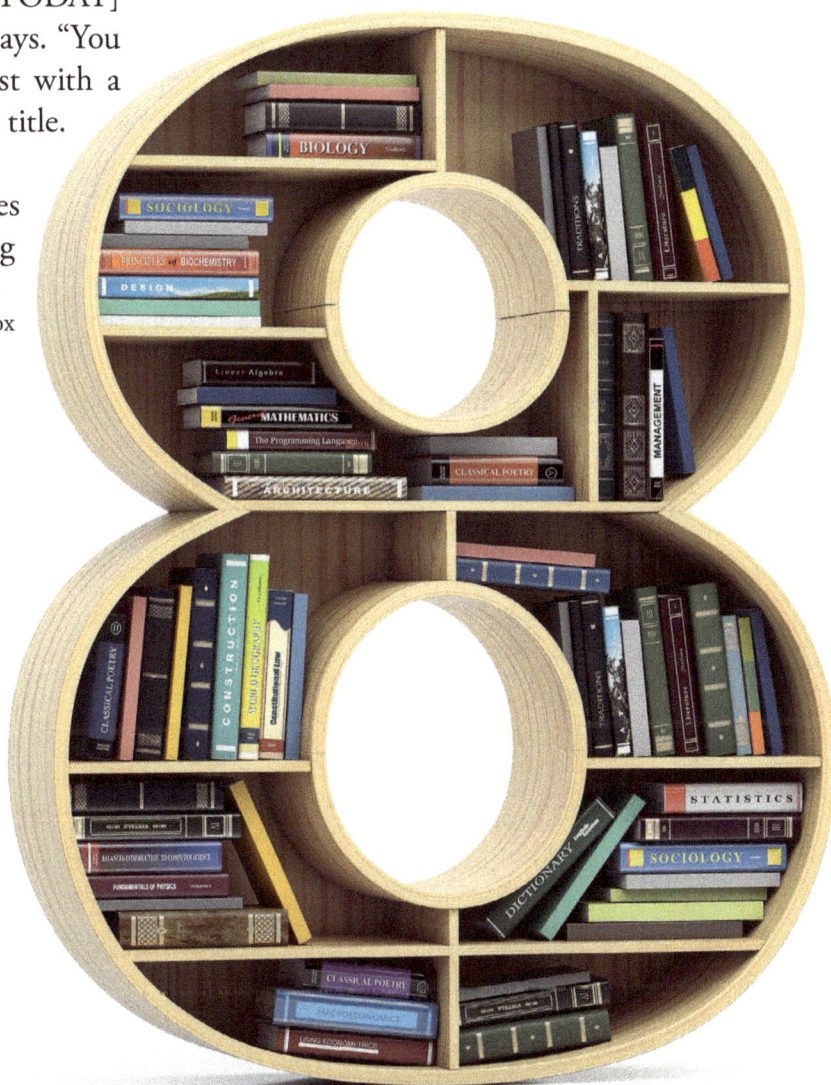

Watching the Clock

HOW TO KEEP TRACK OF TIME IN YOUR WRITING

Whether your manuscript is an epic saga or spans the length of an hour, it's easy to get lost in your own world and lose track of time. You enter the flow excited, sunlight shining through the window, and emerge hours later, exhausted and in the dark.

In the real world, cues like the change in lighting can reorient you pretty quickly, but what happens if you miss those details in your draft? Continuity errors based on confusing timelines can pull readers out of the story and send them searching for missed cues.

For plotters who've worked out every beat but forgotten to note the date, or for pantsers who've followed their characters into a wood too deep to see the stars, there are several ways to get back on track.

INTERNAL TRACKING

Writers with completed drafts may prefer to start with an internal tracking technique, since these often catch clues already built into the manuscript. In some cases, this will be all you need. And even if your internal tracking reveals larger inconsistencies, you can use your notes to build an external tracker before the next revision.

Flags and Annotations: The quickest way to check the flow of time in an existing work is to read through and mark it. You might color code different characters and storylines, but even highlighting the major plot points or circling built-in time references, such as "watching the sunset," "waiting for hours," or "after lunch," will help identify any disruptions in the timeline.

Timestamps: Some writers begin every chapter with a date and time posted at the top. Others add them into revision notations as comments or headings. If a manuscript includes time jumps, flashbacks, or nonlinear storytelling, timestamps can keep the draft organized. Unless the book is a Thriller, however, most authors remove timestamps before publishing, replacing them with embedded references to time passing.

Passage Mapping/Cornell Notes: Passage mapping and Cornell Notes are note-taking methods often used in test prep courses to help students identify significant words and phrases in their reading. The results are a hybrid of annotations and chart building, which can be great for authors who decide they need an outline halfway through writing the novel.

Whereas you can practice passage mapping in the margins of your work, Cornell Notes involve both internal and external documentation. To format them, first read through a chapter, marking

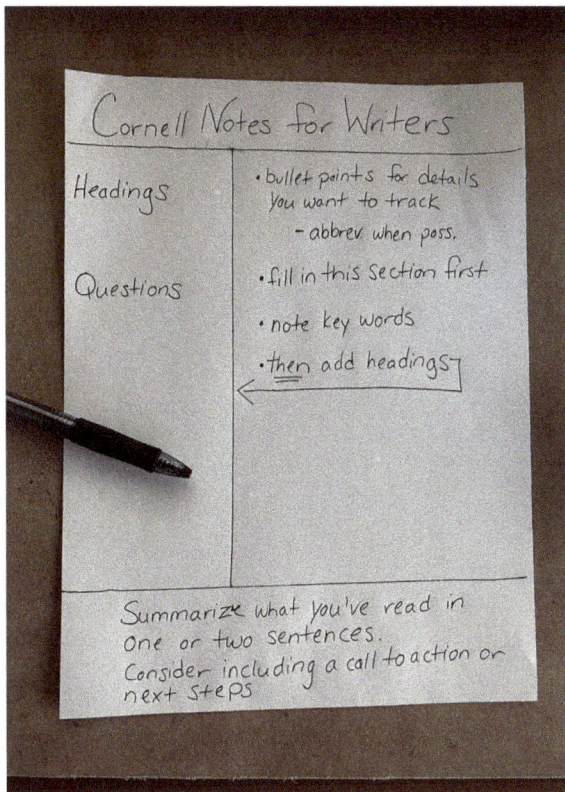

Cornell Notes for Writers

Headings

Questions

- bullet points for details you want to track
  - abbrev when poss.
- fill in this section first
- note key words
- then add headings

Summarize what you've read in one or two sentences. Consider including a call to action or next steps

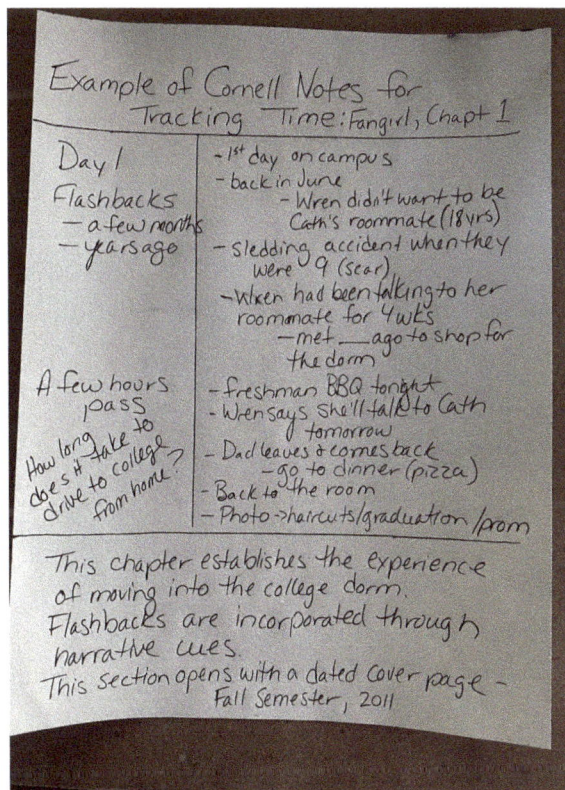

Example of Cornell Notes for Tracking Time: Fangirl, Chapt 1

Day 1
Flashbacks
— a few months
— years ago

- 1st day on campus
- back in June
  - Wren didn't want to be Cath's roommate (18 yrs)
- Sledding accident when they were 9 (scar)
- Wren had been talking to her roommate for 4 wks
  - met ___ ago to shop for the dorm

A few hours pass

- freshman BBQ tonight
- Wren says she'll talk to Cath tomorrow

How long does it take to drive to college from home?

- Dad leaves & comes back
  - go to dinner (pizza)
- Back to the room
- Photo → haircuts/graduation/prom

This chapter establishes the experience of moving into the college dorm. Flashbacks are incorporated through narrative cues. This section opens with a dated cover page - Fall Semester, 2011

any references to time passing, flashbacks, or characters' plans or memories. Then, take abbreviated notes on the events and time references in the right-hand column of my page, and add headings on the left-hand side to identify where these events happen in the story's overall timeline. Jot any timeline questions in the left-hand column as well. At the bottom of the page, write a brief chapter summary. By the end, you'll have an abstract of each chapter and where the events fit into the overall timeline, which you could then use to build an outline.

EXTERNAL TRACKING

These techniques allow writers to keep track of time in a separate document from their work-in-progress and can be created as part of the planning process, constructed and changed during drafting, and/or referenced for revision. As a bonus, external tracking can offer a more visual or tactile organization method than simply color-coding or underlining text.

Timelines, Grids, Charts, and Tables: Timelines are great for organizing big picture events and story mapping. Try using an Excel template, like author Laura Drake suggests in her writing blog (https://writersinthestorm.wordpress.com), a storyboarding program like Plottr to create a digital timeline, or a more in-depth spreadsheet for complex storylines. For a more tactile tool, draw it on a whiteboard or build it on a corkboard with string and Post-It notes. When you need to track multiple timelines or points of view, these options can be more efficient than a series of lists or complex outlines.

Calendars and Planners: If you'd rather lay out events as you would in the real world, find a calendar for the month and year in which your story takes place. Even stories set in the distant past or future can be mapped out using calendars generated online, according to the Aspiring Writing Academy (https://aspiringwriteracademy.com). Alternatively, use an undated planner, especially if the story takes place in a world that doesn't use traditional time tables, like a planet with longer days or a fantasy world that measures time by the sighs of a turtle. Blank planners, like bullet journals, might be more efficient for stories that include large time jumps or fit a significant amount of action into a shorter period.

Outlines and Reverse Outlines: Plotters already know this, but outlining your story in advance is probably the most direct way to make sure that events happen in the order you intend. That doesn't mean that the dreaded formal outline is completely useless to pantsers. You may just have to come at it in reverse.

A reverse outline is exactly what it sounds like: the outline process backwards. After finishing a draft, reread your work, recognizing the natural beats, story arcs, and act breaks. After fitting these into an outline, you can more intentionally arrange details to fit a logical time frame.

Pro Tip: Some writing apps, like Scrivener and Reedsy Book Editor, will do this for you if you set it up before you start writing. Even Microsoft Word and Google Docs have "document outline" features.

Tracking the passage of time tightens pacing and helps authors avoid continuity errors. With so many options, it's easy to incorporate at any stage. Writers who start with an external tracker can still use internal trackers to check their work, and vice versa. So choose a direction, keep your eyes on the path, and you'll find your way out of the woods in no time.

Resources for tracking time:

If you've solved any continuity problems and are looking for ways to show the passage of time more intuitively in your writing, here are a few writers who've shared their methods:

Disha Walia explains how to ace a time skip at https://diymfa.com/writing/ace-a-time-skip

Writer's Edit (https://writersedit.com) offers '5 Ways to Handle Passage of Time'

AJ Humpage breaks down internal time markers at http://allwritefictionadvice.blogspot.com

Nicola Alter looks at alternative ways to measure time in high fantasy at https://thoughtsonfantasy.com

KM Weiland explores eight pros and cons of dramatizing the passage of time in your story at https:/helpingwritersbecomeauthors.com

Jenn Lessmann

How Spicy Romance Authors Turn up the Heat for Readers

Afternoon delight, knocking boots, dancing in the sheets, the horizontal tango—no matter what you want to call it, we all know the lingo. And for some of us, that lingo, and all the colorful acts it represents, can play a big role in the books we write.

Spicy or Steamy Romance covers a range of tastes, from a handful of mild bedroom scenes to "Kindle-melting" levels of heat with all the accompanying implements and inclinations the author can imagine.

But what's needed to consider something a Spicy Romance?

The biggest difference between Romance and Spicy Romance is straightforward: No matter what is going on in the book between the hero and heroine—or any other pairing or number of people in the relationship—the bedroom door stays open. What happens between the participants is described, and the reader gets to see all the details.

If it doesn't have that, it's not a Spicy Romance.

But even there, there are degrees.

DIFFERENT LEVELS OF SPICE OR STEAM

Many Romance review sites have their own ratings for books, usually going from no-sex Romance, with only kissing, right up to the spiciest rating, which includes everything you could imagine—and quite possibly some things you couldn't.

The Shameless Book Club https://shamelessbookclub.com, a book recommendation blog dedicated specifically to steamy stories, offers the following ratings:

One flame, or Feverish, stories include light romance and fade-to-black bedroom scenes.

Two flames, or Fire, stories have some heat without being greatly descriptive.

Three flames, or Molten, stories are "Super hot for adults only."

Four flames, or Nuclear, stories are described as "the hottest of the hot," with encounters that can include dubious consent (dub-con), non-consent (non-con), and/or kink.

There's also often a difference in the language for the different levels. Mildly Spicy Romance will have sex scenes, but what happens is mostly either suggested, described with euphemisms, or otherwise skimmed over. The hotter Romances describe what happens in great detail, with four-letter or other suitable words. The "hottest of the hot," as Shameless puts it, will often contain more graphic descriptions and adult language, along with additions, such as sex toys and other accompaniments.

It's important to keep in mind that book ratings will be different according to each reader's expectations and preferences. Authors shouldn't be surprised if a Spicy Romance novel receives different ratings across reviews, nor should they market their story according to a certain spice level—some readers might find it misleading if the author's rating isn't in line with their own expectations.

Still, no matter what the spice level nor how many bedroom scenes, if it's a Romance, there should always be a proper plot. If a story comprises just sex scenes, then it's gone past Erotic Romance into Erotica.

WHAT ABOUT GENRES, TROPES, AND PAIRINGS?

Spicy Romance has virtually no limit. As long as a story includes romance as a major plot within the story, it can be spicy. A quick look on Amazon brings up spicy options for Sci-Fi Romance with cyborgs and aliens; Contemporary Romance with cowboys, billionaires, mafia, geeks, and the guy or gal next door; Paranormal and Fantasy Romance with monsters, shifters, mythical beings, gods and goddesses, and things that go bump—and grind—in the night; Historical Romance; and even Horror Romance and dinosaurs. Though unless you've invested in a really good eye bleach, can we suggest you not look up that last one on Google?

Pairings really can include whatever floats your boat, including male-male, male-female, female-female, or any combination of any gender. The genre also leaves room for relationships that go beyond monogamy to include multiple partners, ménage, and/or reverse harem, with or without the crossing of "swords and honeypots."

As for tropes, any traditional Romance tropes can work just as well for Spicy Romance. You can find Spicy Romance that are labeled "enemies to lovers," "second-chance romance," "opposites attract," "forced proximity," "fake relationship," "alpha male," and more.

WHAT ELSE TO BE AWARE OF WHEN WRITING SPICY ROMANCE

With romance involved, readers will expect a Happily Ever After (HEA) or Happy For Now (HFN) ending, no matter what else goes on between the pages of the book or how spicy it is.

Apart from that, consent is the biggest thing to watch out for when writing Spicy Romance. Although not everything in every book will be to your or your readers' tastes, there should still be a point in any story where participants consent to what is happening, with some exceptions for dub-con or non-con interactions. However, it doesn't have to be complicated. Something as simple as "Are you okay? Are you sure you want me to *insert hot and sexy description*?" will be fine.

Finally, depending on the themes and plot points in your book, think about whether you need to include a trigger warning. In books with certain dominant characters, for example, there may be more extreme acts, such as play with knives or fire. For some people, such encounters will be right up their alley, but those same descriptions might make other readers uncomfortable. If you know you're including scenes that might be triggering, a short content warning on your back cover copy and inside can be all that's needed to alert people ahead of time.

Liv Honeywell

'Tis the Season To Be Jolly

THREE TIPS FOR FITTING YOUR WRITING TIME INTO THE FESTIVE SEASON

It's that time of year again. Evenings are spent vegging out on the sofa after yet another rich, heavy meal. There are invitations to office parties and family gatherings a-plenty. Food and drink flow freely. Days and nights blend into one another, and normal is a distant memory. The belts around our waists move up a couple of notches, and shops run out of antacid tablets. Welcome back to the holiday season.

Christmas, Thanksgiving, Hanukkah, Kwanzaa—no matter what you celebrate this time of year, for an indie author, holiday celebrations can have harmful effects not only on your bottom but also on your bottom line. You may decide to put all thoughts of writing and promotion aside for a few days, weeks, or months. But if you want to stay writing fit, here are our top tips for getting through the season.

1. Set boundaries: Be upfront with your family, your friends, and yourself. Set crystal-clear goals ahead of time for how much you plan to write or what your world count will be daily, but remember, it is sensible to set lower targets compared with your normal output. This will allow you to join in with all the festive fun and still spend time on your business. You can have your pumpkin pie and eat it too.

2. Be kind: All work and no play makes Jack a dull boy. No one wants to see or hear you moaning about getting back to your book. When you are partying, party. When you are supposed to be writing, write. Your time is yours to manage. Staying at your desk rather than joining your little ones under the tree on Christmas Day is not

good for your creative soul. Be generous to yourself and others. If you missed your word count, don't take it out on the people you love. Get up earlier the next day and catch up on your own time.

3. Stay healthy: Your brain needs fuel to work, so stay hydrated, and get out in the fresh air. Alcohol, too many sugary snacks, or creamy sauces can play havoc with more than your waistline. As a writer, you probably already live a mainly sedentary lifestyle, so make the most of being untethered from your desk and go for a walk after meals. Play physically active games with those presents you bought for your kids, and dance yourself silly every night. It is the holiday season, after all.

Susan Odev

Stop the World–I Want to Write!

WITH THE RIGHT MINDSET, STORYTELLING OFFERS SANCTUARY AND AN ANSWER TO DOOMSCROLLING

Turn on the news. Read a paper. Scroll through social media. No matter where you go, it's hard to avoid today's world. It seeps in through your pores even when you try your best to switch everything off. Go to the grocery store, and mawkish headlines greet you near the entrance. On the radio, advertisements yell at you to be better, buy this miracle drug, or vote this way because you can't trust the other guy. Sadly, it's rarely uplifting. The twenty-first century invites the pain and suffering of others to take a seat beside us on our couches at night or join us for cereal over breakfast. We do not confine fear and loathing to Las Vegas anymore. It's omnipresent.

Yet, as a writer, you are among the blessed few who can use their work to pull the virtual shutters and leave it all behind. Many people think you need solitude to craft words into the magic that is a fresh new book, but all you need is focus. Just as your readers can turn to your well-honed words to escape, you can use the act of writing as your safe haven too.

The world today offers plenty of distractions, but these same platforms can also provide effective tools you can use to hide yourself away. Ambient videos on YouTube can offer respite from the real world and a chance to listen to the sounds of Victorian England or a medieval apothecary. There are videos for every conceivable destination in time and space. Plug in your noise-canceling headphones, transport your senses to a different place, and allow your words, and your imagination, to do the rest.

Make your writing a fully immersive experience. Turn off your notifications, and plug yourself into whatever background vibe works for you. Close your eyes, and allow yourself to wander your own streets. Make small talk with elves or gangsters. Stand on your own mountaintop at midnight, sing to your own stars, chase your own purple waterfalls—whatever floats your boat. Your stories are your refuge from reality and of your own design.

Susan Odev

CRAFT

Put It All Together Now

GROW YOUR AUDIENCE AND YOUR PUBLISHING SKILLS BY ORGANIZING ANTHOLOGIES

Are you an author who likes to volunteer your time for a good cause, find mentors, learn from your peers, or learn by doing? By organizing an anthology for your target audience, you can not only build your publishing skills and the audience for your books but also share the voices of other authors with new readers. Depending on your goals, you could even make the world a little better with your art.

But if you're taking on the role of team leader, there are some things you should keep in mind before you get started.

CHARITY

The indie publishing world has a big heart. Anthologies offer some of the best examples of this—several authors choose to organize their first anthologies for a good cause, including Fantasy and Post-Apocalypse author J.A. Clement. For those who've entered a few anthologies as a participant and are ready for the next step, organizing a charitable anthology could be a good starting place, Clement writes. They "can be as simple as twenty authors putting in [three thousand] words each, volunteering their production skills, and then making a couple of hundred quid for a relevant charity. It might be small scale but … you're learning the same skills you'll need later … in a lower-stress environment."

There are practical benefits too: Having a common goal inspires authors to get involved, and it simplifies the accounting. You wouldn't need to worry about dividing royalties since you would donate the lump sum to a single account.

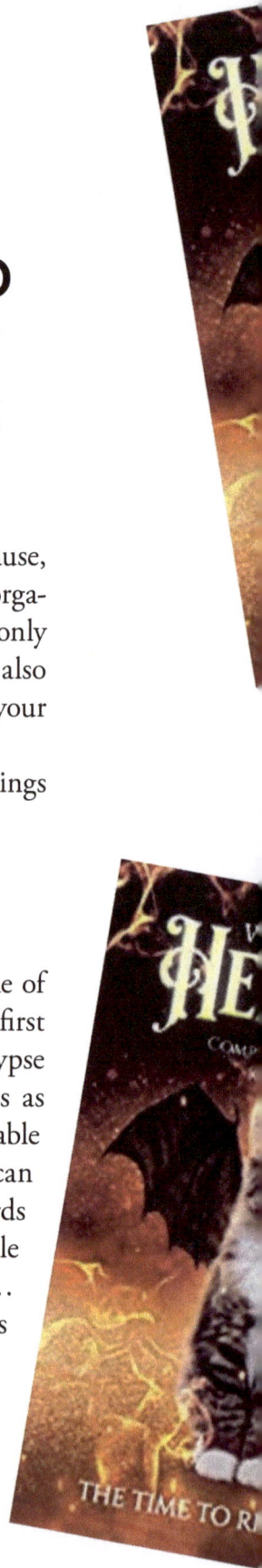

64 | Indie Author Magazine · December 2022

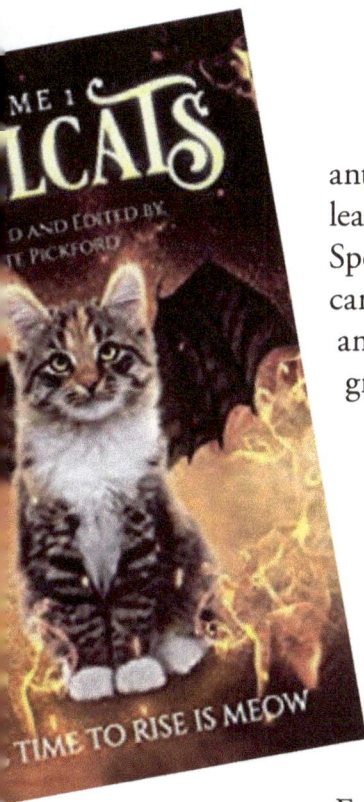

Of course, there's more than one path to organizing your own anthology, and being involved with author groups may naturally lead to more collaboration. For Lasairiona McMaster, a steamy Sports Romance author, her entrance into the world of anthologies came when someone volunteered her to co-organize a Romance anthology in the 20BooksTo50K® Facebook group. Sometimes greatness is thrust upon you.

CLARITY

Clement, who has served as "facilitatrix" for multiauthor teams, takes her responsibilities more seriously than her title. "Anyone who is helping you with something is part of [your] team," she writes. "These are [your] people and it is your responsibility to make sure no-one is bullied, talked down to, discriminated against, or otherwise made to feel bad. Everyone has the right to do their work with dignity and some basic respect."

Planning, setting deadlines that don't clash with one another, matching tasks to skills and interests as much as possible, staying in touch with everyone, and celebrating small and big wins are all responsibilities that fall on the shoulders of any anthology organizer and can make the difference between a thriving, excited team and a debacle. "Make sure you have one person for them all [the writers] to report to," Clement suggests, "so that nothing gets lost or too far out of timetable."

Don't forget creative boundaries either. Robyn Sarty, Thriller author and publisher of several Fairy-Tale Retelling anthologies, recommends making genre expectations clear from the beginning, "especially if you want to go deep into your subniche." And when working with a team of editors or co-organizers, Clement suggests deciding upfront "who gets the final say on edits, or the cover."

Managing so many responsibilities is a lot for anyone to take on. It's important to pay attention to self-care throughout the process. "Going into collaboration can be very powerful, but it can also be exhausting," Clement writes. "Bear in mind that you're going to have to give up some of the freedoms that make self-publishing attractive, because other people will now be involved."

CONTRACTS

Anthologies can be great fun, but it's essential to remember that you're entering a business venture with anyone you bring onto your team—even close friends. "A contract is key," Sarty writes. "It doesn't have to be complicated, but it … takes the strain off of responsibilities and expectations."

Contracts may include word limits, themes, formatting, deadlines, marketing and social media commitments, cost and royalty sharing, duration of the collaboration, and when authors can expect print, digital, and audio rights to revert to them. Remember to include any creative boundaries in your contracts.

Sarty recommends starting with a template contract like the one in Craig Martelle's Successful Indie Author Collaborations. As for putting it into practice, Clement recommends using Basecamp project management software (https://basecamp.com) if the budget allows, or free tools like Google Docs or Dropbox if it doesn't, to communicate and to keep track of submissions. Again, this is an area where planning will make you and your team much happier, she writes. We've all been in that last-minute indie publishing crunch for our own projects at least once, and none of us want to do that with our team watching us, she writes. "It's really miserable if you're left scrambling to meet a deadline on a brand new programme where you have no idea how it works," Clement writes.

For a charitable anthology, you may not need to calculate royalty shares. But if you want to organize an anthology where the royalties will be split, you can choose to divide costs and royalties in numerous ways. Sarty's publishing company covered editing, cover design, and marketing costs. McMaster took care of the cover and asked authors to "chip in for paid promo site newsletters" when they discounted the anthology. Clement prefers to divide up the royalties based on each collaborator's work: "a percentage for those involved in the actual production work, and the remainder split either equally or according to word count." The author and organizer points out the risks of paying off costs over time with royalties. "Anthologies can make a couple of grand, but if you want more, it requires a considerable marketing budget or an insanely

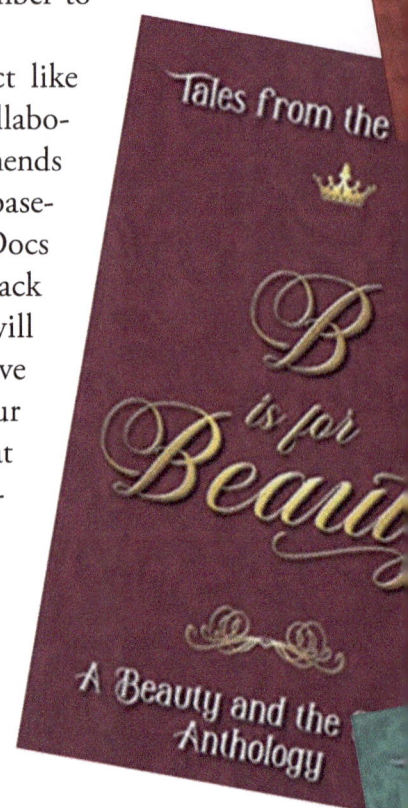

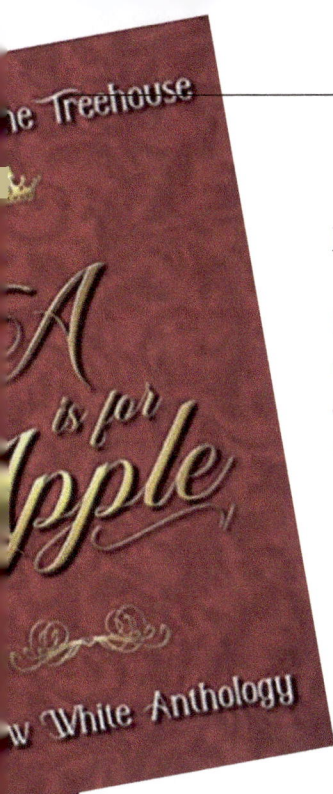

large number of contributors and a very good cause," she writes.

Splitting royalties can be complex, but there are tools to help. Depending on if and how you plan to pay your team members, tools like Draft2Digital's payment splitting tool can automatically divide royalties among collaborators. "Depending on how you want to organize this box set … the organizer, is going to get—this might be unfair, but maybe they're getting 50 percent and … the second 50 percent is being split among the contributors," said Kevin Tumlinson, director of marketing and PR at Draft-2Digital, in a February 2021 interview for the podcast Self Publishing Insiders. "You can set all that up, and it's all automated. Taxes are all taken care of." Mark Leslie Lefebvre, also of Draft2Digital, noted in the same interview that the tool saves organizers from excess foreign exchange fees for collaborations with international authors and can also send required tax documents to collaborators.

Draft2Digital isn't an organizer's only option; other programs offer similar services for dividing royalty shares across several price ranges. PubShare (https://pubshare.com)—previously known as BundleRabbit—charges 10 percent of the income to divide royalties as set by the organizer. PublishDrive (https://publishdrive.zendesk.com) offers two royalty splitting tools, a calculator called "PD Abacus" for $2.99 per month that can be used by authors who don't have a PublishDrive subscription and "Team Royalties," which require all authors to have a PublishDrive subscription and pay an additional monthly fee of $19.99 per "seat." According to PublishDrive's site: "The number of seats determines how many different co-authors you can have invited at the same time. One seat means a spot for one co-author who can be invited to unlimited teams. You can change who the co-author is without adding extra seats."

For long-term royalty splitting, new technology is on the horizon. In a July 2022 interview with Roanie Levy of Access Copyright (https://accesscopyright.ca/), Joanna Penn of The Creative Penn podcast pointed out the value of blockchain technology. "One of the things that stops authors collaborating is that it's so hard to do all of these royalty payments later on in the process. If you and I write a book together, one of us will publish it or we'll get a publisher and then the money eventually gets to us or one of us has to split

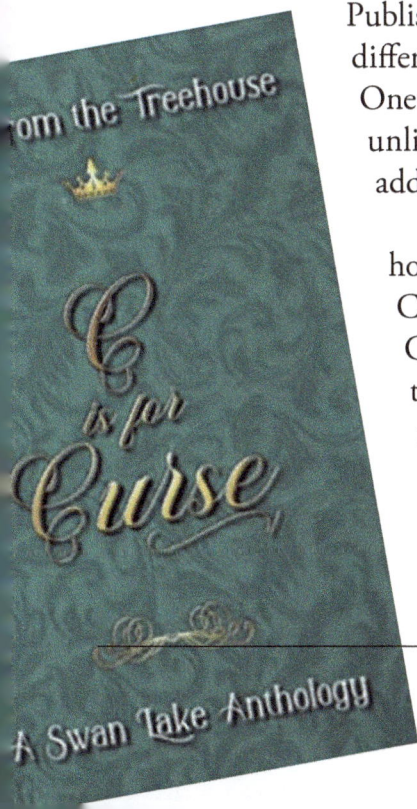

it," Penn said. "With a smart contract … there can be a percentage for the fan who's selling it that can be a percentage [that] goes back to the original creator or creators and a percentage could go to a charity, for example. … [Even] after my death … there's a clause in the contract that will redirect the payments to a different wallet."

COLLABORATION

Organizing more concrete details in an anthology ahead of time, like deadlines and royalty shares, is critical, but McMaster also recommends thinking about "alignment" early in the process. "You need … a clear idea of the purpose and goals of the anthology, and a solid knowledge of your subgenre," she writes.

Authors may join an anthology to contribute to charity, build their skills, apprentice with more experienced authors or organizers, grow a broader audience for their work, improve their "also boughts," or increase their income. Keeping this combination of goals in mind will help you and your team get the most from the experience.

As Clement puts it, "There's a great deal of excitement in being part of a high-performing team; but also, perseverance and tolerance is needed from everyone for the bumpy bits of the road. So choose your team and make sure everyone has their expectations set the same."

CONNECTION

Anthologies offer opportunities for creativity and connection with other professionals and readers. Once you've deliberately practiced the skills you need for a successful collaboration, you can keep growing your publishing business and your audience with shared worlds, co-authoring, bundling, more anthologies, or publishing other authors.

Clement offers a final word of advice to those interested who haven't yet published others' work. "Forming a publishing house

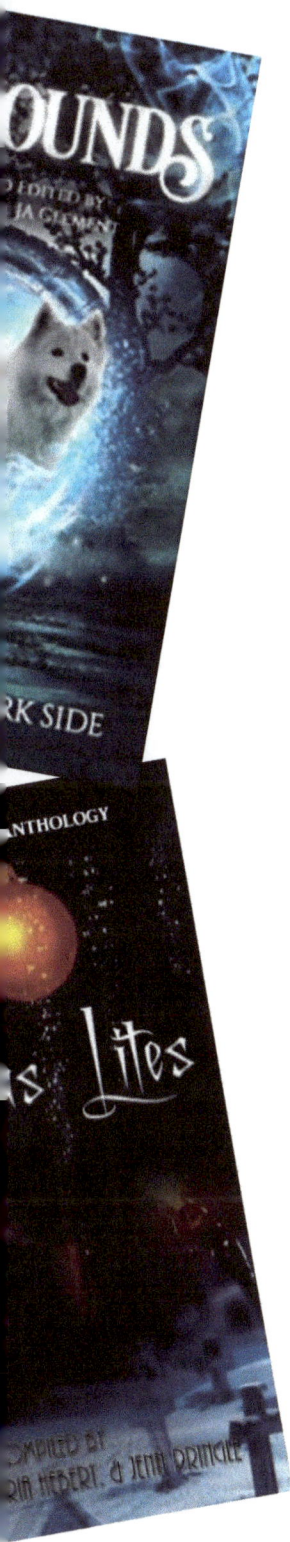

is quite hardcore," she writes. "I should say that's something for people who only want to write a couple of books but love the process. It requires a bit of self awareness. Experiment with the things you really excel at and the things you really enjoy; if that's the production or marketing side more than the writing then it may be something to look into. … I'd start small with a couple of low key anthologies, [then] scale it up and see how you get on with the people-wrangling."

Resources

For tips on bundling, co-authoring, and anthologies, read Get Your Book Selling with Cross-Promotion by Monica Leonelle. For sample contracts for collaborative work with other authors, check out Successful Indie Author Collaborations by Craig Martelle.

For more anthologies to join and/or study, visit Facebook groups like Wide Anthology, Boxed Sets, & Shared Worlds/Brands Collaboration Group or Margo's Group for Authors–Boxed Sets.

Select Anthologies by J.A. Clement, Robyn Sarty, and Lasairiona McMaster:

- Hellhounds: Anthology, organized by Kate Pickford and J.A. Clement
- Hellcats Anthology: Volume 1, organized by Kate Pickford
- Hellcats Anthology: Volume 2, organized by Kate Pickford
- A is for Apple: A Snow White Anthology, organized by Robyn Sarty and Belwood Publishing
- B is for Beauty: A Beauty and the Beast Anthology, organized by Robyn Sarty and Belwood Publishing
- C is for Curse: A Swan Lake Anthology, organized by Robyn Sarty and Belwood Publishing
- Christmas Lites series of anthologies for the National Coalition for Domestic Violence, organized by J.A. Clement

Laurel Decher

In This Issue

Executive Team

Chelle Honiker, Publisher

As the publisher of Indie Author Magazine, Chelle Honiker brings nearly three decades of startup, technology, training, and executive leadership experience to the role. She's a serial entrepreneur, founding and selling multiple successful companies including a training development company, travel agency, website design and hosting firm, a digital marketing consultancy, and a wedding planning firm. She's organized and curated multiple TEDx events and hired to assist other nonprofit organizations as a fractional executive, including The Travel Institute and The Freelance Association.

As a writer, speaker, and trainer she believes in the power of words and their ability to heal, inspire, incite, and motivate. Her greatest inspiration is her daughters, Kelsea and Cathryn, who tolerate her tendency to run away from home to play with her friends around the world for months at a time. It's said she could run a small country with just the contents of her backpack.

Alice Briggs, Creative Director

As the creative director of Indie Author Magazine, Alice Briggs utilizes her more than three decades of artistic exploration and expression, business startup adventures, and leadership skills. A serial entrepreneur, she has started several successful businesses. She brings her experience in creative direction, magazine layout and design, and graphic design in and outside of the indie author community to her role.

With a masters of science in Occupational Therapy, she has a broad skill set and uses it to assist others in achieving their desired goals. As a writer, teacher, healer, and artist, she loves to see people accomplish all they desire. She's excited to see how IAM will encourage many authors to succeed in whatever way they choose. She hopes to meet many of you in various places around the world once her passport is back in use.

Nicole Schroeder, Editor in Chief

Nicole Schroeder is a storyteller at heart. As the editor in chief of Indie Author Magazine, she brings nearly a decade of journalism and editorial experience to the publication, delighting in any opportunity to tell true stories and help others do the same. She holds a bachelor's degree from the Missouri School of Journalism and minors in English and Spanish. Her previous work includes editorial roles at local publications, and she's helped edit and produce numerous fiction and nonfiction books, including a Holocaust survivor's memoir, alongside independent publishers. Her own creative writing has been published in national literary magazines. When she's not at her writing desk, Nicole is usually in the saddle, cuddling her guinea pigs, or spending time with family. She loves any excuse to talk about Marvel movies and considers National Novel Writing Month its own holiday.

Writers

Laurel Decher

There might be no frigate like a book, but publishing can feel like a voyage on the H.M.S. Surprise. There's always a twist and there's never a moment to lose.

Laurel's mission is to help you make the most of today's opportunities. She's a strategic problem-solver, tool collector, and co-inventor of the "you never know" theory of publishing.

As an epidemiologist, she studied factors that help babies and toddlers thrive. Now she writes books for children ages nine to twelve about finding more magic in life. She's a member of the Society for Children's Book Writers and Illustrators (SCBWI), has various advanced degrees, and a tendency to smuggle vegetables into storylines.

Gill Fernley

Gill Fernley writes fiction in several genres under different pen names, but what all of them have in common is humour and romance, because she can't resist a happy ending or a good laugh. She's also a freelance content writer and has been running her own business since 2013. Before that, she was a technical author and documentation manager for an engineering company and can describe to you more than you'd ever wish to know about airflow and filtration in downflow booths. Still awake? Wow, that's a first! Anyway, that experience taught her how to explain complex things in straightforward language and she hopes it will come in handy for writing articles for IAM. Outside of writing, she's a cake decorator, expert shoe hoarder, and is fluent in English, dry humour and procrastibaking.

Audrey Hughey

Audrey Hughey designs planners, writes fiction, and works diligently to help her fellow authors. Although she currently writes horror and thrillers, she's as eclectic in her writing tastes as in her reading. When she's not submerged in the worlds of fiction and nonfiction, she's caring for her family, enjoying nature, or finding more ways to bring a little more light into the world.

Jenn Lessmann

Jenn Lessmann is the author of three stories published on Amazon's Kindle Vella, two unpublished novels, and a blog that tests Pinterest hacks in the real world (where supplies are sometimes limited, and all projects are overseen by children with digital attention spans). A former barista, stage manager, and high school English teacher with advanced degrees from impressive colleges, she continues to drink excessive amounts of caffeine, stay up later than is absolutely necessary, and read three or four books at a time. She loves lists and the rule of three. Irony too. Jenn is currently studying witchcraft and the craft of writing, and giggling internally whenever they intersect. She writes snarky (not spicy) paranormal fantasy for new adults whenever her dog will allow it.

When she's not writing, you can find Kasia scouting out the best coffee shops in town, planning her next great adventure, or petting other people's puppies.

Megan Linski-Fox

Megan Linski lives in Michigan. She is a USA TODAY Bestselling Author and the author of more than fifty novels. She has over fifteen years of experience writing books alongside working as a journalist and editor. She graduated from the University of Iowa, where she studied Creative Writing.

Megan advocates for the rights of the disabled, and is an activist for mental health awareness. She co-writes the Hidden Legends Universe with Alicia Rades. She also writes under the pen name of Natalie Erin for the Creatures of the Lands series, co-authored by Krisen Lison.

Craig Martelle

High school Valedictorian enlists in the Marine Corps under a guaranteed tank contract. An inauspicious start that was quickly superseded by excelling in language study. Contract waived, a year at the Defense Language Institute to learn Russian and off to keep my ears on the big red machine during the Soviet years. Back to DLI for advanced Russian after reenlisting. Deploying. Then getting selected to get a commission. Earned a four-year degree in two years by majoring in Russian Language. It was a cop out, but I wanted to get back to the fleet.

One summa cum laude graduation later, that's where I found myself. My first gig as a second lieutenant was on a general staff. I did well enough that I stayed at that level or higher for the rest of my career, while getting some choice side gigs – UAE, Bahrain, Korea, Russia, and Ukraine.

Major Martelle. I retired from the Marines after a couple years at the embassy in Moscow working arms control issues. The locals called me The German, because of my accent in Russian. That worked for me. It kept me off the radar. Just until it didn't. Expelled after two years for activities inconsistent with my diplomatic status, I went to Ukraine. Can't let twenty years of Russian language go to waste. More arms control. More diplomatic stuff. Then 9/11 and off to war. That was enough deployment for me. Then came retirement.

Department of Homeland Security was a phenomenally miserable gig. I quit that job quickly enough and went to law school. A second summa cum laude later and I was working for a high-end consulting firm performing business diagnostics, business law, and leadership coaching. More deployments. For the money they paid me, I was good with that. Just until I wasn't. Then I started writing. You'll find Easter eggs from my career hidden within all my books. Enjoy the stories.

Kevin McLaughlin

Kevin McLaughlin is the USA Today bestselling author of 83 books. He writes mostly science fiction and fantasy, and is also the author of The Coffee Break Novelist and You Must Write. He's enjoyed reading and writing serials for decades.

Susan Odev

Susan has banked over three decades of work experience in the fields of personal and organizational development, being a freelance corporate trainer and consultant alongside holding down "real" jobs for over twenty-five years. Specializing in entrepreneurial mindsets, she has written several non-fiction business books, once gaining a coveted Amazon #1 best seller tag in business and entrepreneurship, an accolade she now strives to emulate with her fiction.

Currently working on her fifth novel, under a top secret pen name, the craft and marketing aspects of being a successful indie author equally fascinate and terrify her.

A lover of history with a criminal record collection, Susan lives in a retro orange and avocado world. Once described by a colleague as being an "onion," Susan has many layers, as have ogres (according to Shrek). She would like to think this makes her cool, her teenage children just think she's embarrassing.

Kristin Rodin

Kristin Rodin is a senior journalism major graduating from Texas Tech University December 2022. She's always loved writing and connecting with her community, ans is beyond thankful to have the opportunity to do both as a career. Outside of work, she loves crocheting, volunteering, and spending time with her dog, Hazel. After college, she plans to pursue healthcare communication to make health information more accessible to her community.

Ready to level up your indie author career?

Trick question. Of course you are.

*INDIE
^Author Tools

Get Your Friday Five Newsletter and find your next favorite tool here.

https://writelink.to/iat

Join the Facebook group here.

https://writelink.to/iatfb

PUBLISHER ROCKET

FIND
PROFITABLE
KINDLE
KEYWORDS

Book Marketing Research
Made Simple!

writelink.to/pubrocket

www.ingramcontent.com/pod-product-compliance
Lightning Source LLC
Chambersburg PA
CBHW052344210326
41597CB00037B/6255